RESILIENT FAITH

DARE TO BELIEVE

Compiled by

Rhonda P. Fraser

Resilient Faith: Dare to Believe

Published by R. Frasers Connection, LLC.

2021912998

Library of Congress Cataloging-in-Publication Data is available

ISBN 978-1-7368632-0-6

ISBN 978-1-7368632-3-7 (ebook)

Dedication

This book is specially dedicated back to God. He is the One who has inspired me to produce it for His glory! I am forever grateful for His eternal love, grace, and blessing upon my life and my family.

Special dedication and thank you to every contributing author for your faith-building stories. You are such an inspiration to the world. My hope is that these stories would strengthen the faith of the readers and become a great resource for the Kingdom of God.

Special dedication to my husband, Reginald; sons, Raphael and Reginald Jr. (RJ); daughter, Rebecca, and my mother, Evelyn. Thank you for giving me the love and support that makes life so meaningful. You are all amazing and loved very much.

Get ready to walk in Resilient Faith and Dare to Believe God!

Rhonda

Table of Contents

Foreword

I am delighted to write this foreword for my wife Rhonda P. Fraser, affectionately known as Rhonnie. Before we got married in 1988 to today, I have observed her constant faith and love for God and people. She wears all her hats well: wife, mother, daughter, sister, friend, leader; both secularly and in ministry. I love the way she balances life, even in difficult times. I personally witnessed her strength as a caregiver for several years, for my elderly mother who had some health challenges.

Her passion for empowering others, especially women, is admirable. She is grounded in her faith in God, yet she is able to reach people from all spectrums of life, regardless of demographics. That is why I believe everyone will connect with some chapter in this book.

Women are very important in transmitting the message of faith, hope, and love. They were the first ones who saw and communicated that message when Jesus resurrected from the grave. They play a very important role in society and in the Kingdom of

God. I know their strength – I was raised by one, my dear mother, Yvonne Fraser, who was very instrumental in who I am today.

Rhonda has chosen some amazing women leaders to come alongside her in writing this outstanding book, including her faithful mother, Mom Evelyn. They have all been able to wonderfully communicate the message of faith in shaping our destiny.

I believe that this faith guidebook will propel you to your God-given purpose. It will become one of your best assets and a precious gift to everyone who secures one.

Enjoy your faith journey!

Rev. Reginald Fraser

Introduction

Author Rhonda P. Fraser

The year 2020 has ushered in an onslaught of insurmountable turmoil, especially with the pandemic and other agitations around the world. Every day people are battling some crisis in the home or externally - whether it be financial, health-related, relational, or otherwise. How do we withstand these pressures and still fulfill our purpose? While some situations are clearly out of our control, there is much positive transformation that could occur by making a firm decision of faith.

Life is constantly proving to us that the choices we make today, will shape our tomorrow. From the moment we awake to the time we retire to bed, decision-making and faith activities are impacting our lives. The thinking process is one part of the equation; accepting those thoughts and acting upon them are the critical follow-up steps. We get to choose which thoughts to embrace; which ones to refute and our response to every encounter. Yes, we get to decide where our mind, body, and spirit will take us every day.

It is said that whatever we do consistently for a month becomes a habit, which could influence our way of life. A good exercise is to intentionally track your thinking patterns and subsequent actions for the next thirty days, and observe the direction of your life. That discovery should indicate where you need to make the necessary adjustments for a healthier outcome.

Faith is at work in our daily lives, many times unconsciously. For instance, when we connect with people, we presume reliability; when we utilize products and services, we expect the functionality as projected.

Here are a few examples of faith decisions that we make routinely and may take for granted. When we sit on a chair, we believe it will hold us up; when we use our phones, we expect connectivity; when we get into a vehicle, we believe that we will arrive safely at our destination. To further examine the last scenario, it is remarkable that we are inadvertently placing trust in a number of components. We are putting confidence in the maker of that vehicle; the service team; the driver; other drivers on the road and their vehicles; the road maintenance team; the GPS guide, and an extensive list of factors. We are trusting that everyone is reliably handling their obligation.

I remember showing a co-worker the photos of the wreckage of an accident in 2014, involving my two sons. As expected, she was amazed that they both, not only survived, but walked away without a scratch. She was the owner of a similar model car, so her elated takeaway was, "the car lived up to its great reputation in protecting its occupants." I agreed with her to an extent, but my summation was somewhat different.

Clearly, the work of darkness was behind the scenes, but my sons' assignment on earth was not completed at that time, and God intervened. I recall after they drove off that day, I was engaged in extensive faith-filled prayers and praises to God. Five minutes before the accident occurred, the Lord nudged my husband into a faith-projected prayer for them. The plan of the enemy that day to interrupt their purpose was thwarted.

The important lesson for life is this: even after placing confidence in man's promise, there is still Someone greater with final authority. He is the One with supreme responsibility who knows everything about us; our mission and its expiration.

Therefore, our position of faith is to align with His purpose and reject the plans of the enemy.

Our confidence has to be in more than the maker of possessions; or in people, systems and places. Our assurance has to be in our Maker, Sustainer, and Savior. It is Him who gives us the breath of life. The Bible reminds us in Psalm 31:15, "my times are in Your hands (NKJV)." He is the One who is equipped to get us safely to our destination (our purpose) both here on earth and our eternal destination.

Our reliance on Him is inadvertently at work every night when we go to bed. We have no control over what happens after we fall asleep. We are unconsciously putting our trust in Him who knows it all. When we draft our plans for the following day(s), faith is activated; we are believing that He will wake us up to accomplish those plans. When we take those first steps out of bed, we are instinctively believing that our legs will support us and continue to do so throughout the day. It is evident that we are continuously putting faith in someone or something. Most importantly, we are ultimately relying on the Almighty One, whether we believe it or not, whether we are aware of it or not; whether we believe in Him or not.

This book will not only sharpen your awareness of those daily faith movements; it will take you one step further in enlightening you to the power of receiving and applying resilient faith. You will hear true stories of women, whose lives were changed based on their decision to intentionally walk that faith journey through very challenging times. Many of them found healing, deliverance, provision - purpose - MIRACLES, even in dead-end situations. After reading this book, YOU TOO will be ready to make that decision of faith that gets you to your purpose – to your destination. Join me on this venture to step out in faith and DARE TO BELIEVE GOD!

CHAPTER 1

Author Rhonda P. Fraser

Stepping in Faith and over Fear

Author Rhonda P. Fraser

Children teach us some lifelong lessons! I am always amazed at the persistence of toddlers whenever I see them learning to walk. They do not become expert walkers on their first attempt, but their determination to keep trying until they master the skill is a perfect picture of resiliency. Their pursuit of walking is never abandoned because of those difficult, scary first steps, which oftentimes include missteps, trips, and falls. They just keep stepping in faith and over fear, knowing that someone dependable and supportive is nearby watching and encouraging them to keep going.

Like children, who trust their caretaker, when we place complete trust in the Lord, our Maker, we too become courageous in our faith steps. We rely on His watchful eye, encouragement and support through every hill and valley experience. We have the assurance that He is capable of handling anything we encounter and He knows exactly what He is doing.

It takes faith to accomplish our God-given mission. Hebrews 11:6 informs us that "…without faith, it is impossible to please Him (NKJV)." That is why we have to directly confront the monster of fear, which is the opponent of faith. The two cannot coexist. In 2 Timothy 1:7, we are reminded that "…God has not given us a spirit of fear, but of power, love and a sound mind (NKJV)." So, if fear was not given to us by God, then its origin is obvious. It is a tool of the enemy to manipulate us.

Fear cripples us. It threatens our confidence in God and prevents us from progressing in our assignment. Have you ever wondered what could be accomplished if fear was not a hindrance, especially in current times with intensified trepidation? There is the fear of rejection; fear of being hurt; fear of loss; fear of failure - fear of the unknown!

Indeed, many people go through unbelievable, unfair, and heart-wrenching situations. Being on the receiving end of lies; betrayal; rejection; abandonment; abuse; loss; lack; sickness, stress, and overall hardships, could sometimes shake our trust. However, we cannot allow these circumstances, and the constant frightful reports in society, to confine our trajectory. We are not subjected to man's predication over our lives; we respond to God's report – God's plan, God's way!

There were times in my life where I personally had to reject the negative expectations of others, including adverse reports by experts. The onus is on each of us to preserve our faith and not accept the limitations of man, which are bondages of the adversary. We have to break those restrictions, tear down those strongholds and embrace God's design. It may mean refusing to settle; starting over; partnering with faith-filled people; and sometimes embracing solitude for a period to focus and draw strength for the journey.

I recall a particular negative report on my life as a young married woman. This was a medical report given by a doctor that indicated that there would be no biological children in our future. The burden of worry was constantly trying to disturb my peace, until the day I said, "that's enough!" I refused to continue to live under that dread and was ready to embrace only what God had for me; nothing more, nothing less! My faith was ready to accept only God's blueprint – whatever that meant. When we are truly ready to come into alignment with God's plan and ignore naysayers, we find peace and see breakthroughs!

Our beautiful children; two sons and a daughter, proved that God is not subjected to man's report and He still performs miracles. Some miracles happen immediately, others take a while. Our first son came seven years after marriage and our second son came seventeen years after marriage; both with pregnancy complications and lots or bedrest. My daughter, on the other hand, arrived twenty-one years after marriage, in my forties, with reports of possible high risks, but none of those threats materialized. Unlike her brothers, my pregnancy with her was very easy and with absolutely no complications, but it took a long time for that promise to come to pass. We have the assurance that whatever God promises, whatever He has for us, He is able to perform, regardless of how long it takes. Glory to the Promise Keeper! God gives us peace and patience in the waiting process. Patience is a benefit of our faith journey. James 1:3 explains it well, "knowing that the testing of your faith produces patience (NKJV)." What an amazing gain from our challenges – Patience! It is a part of the fruit of the Spirit explained in the scriptures in Galatians. It exudes God's peace. Most of us have been exposed to the anxiety that impatience brings. We see it every day in the way people interact with each other, especially hurried drivers on the road. If we are not alert and intentional in being calm, we could be swooped up in this anxious current. One of the underlying elements of impatience is fear, which often results in impulsive decisions outside of God's plan.

We cannot be so fearful that we find ourselves far removed from the will of God. There is God's permissive will and there is His perfect will. In 1 Samuel 8, we see God allowing His permissive will for the people who requested an earthly king, but His perfect plan was to be their Heavenly King. We need to strive for His plan;

which gives us peace. Proverbs 10:22, makes it clear that "the blessings of the Lord make us rich and adds no sorrow (NKJV)."

Many times, our peace is attacked by negative reports. While we cannot be naïve and ignore the warnings and help of professionals, we have to leave room for God's plan and not be so quick to succumb to whatever is thrown our way. The intuition that God placed within us often guides us to make decisions that may be difficult to explain to others. Even when the outcome is not what we expect, there is peace that a greater move of God is happening which often becomes clearer in hindsight. Do not give up on your promise from God because of the length of time it is taking or based on the complications of your story. God's promise is still alive and could evolve at a time when you least expect it, and sometimes in the most unusual ways. Keep an open mind.

Society projects a negative report of the outcome of children of single mothers who grew up with limited resources. The statistics show a high probability of them getting into all sorts of trouble and sometimes having unproductive lives. My faith in God gave me the determination to reject that report. In addition, my mother's faith would never allow me to accept thoughts of being marginalized, although, sometimes she struggled financially as a single woman. She insisted on the benefits of quality education, but most importantly, a relationship with Jesus, supported by a home filled with love. It is her guidance that helped me to understand how God wastes nothing in our lives. He connects all of our experiences from every season and molds it all together into our mission on earth. I am forever indebted to her for those structural pillars. I strongly believe that our wellbeing in life is often connected to the way we honor the one who bore us and the one(s) who took care of us. I shared how my mom's life impacted most of what I do today and the importance of believing the report of the Lord, in the bestseller books that I co-authored: *"Women of War: Peace in the Midst of the Storm"*, compiled by Dr. Delene Musielak, and *"This Is How I Fight My Battles"* compiled by Kenise Etwaru.

One of the most important lessons mom taught me is that our faith is not restricted to specific days or places. We do not walk in it on Sunday alone at church; our faith expands to every day and every aspect of our lives - our home; our vocation and other commitments during the week. It takes courage to navigate those different dimensions. I love the scripture, Joshua 1:9 that says, "Have I not commanded you? Be strong and courageous. Do not be afraid; do not be discouraged; for the Lord your God will be with you wherever you go (NKJV)."

There were so many leaders in Bible times who were faithful in their roles at work while honoring God. Some of them were even in places of prominence, like Deborah, Esther, Daniel and Joseph, to name a few. Could it be that God has placed you in that position at that organization because He is relying on you to make sound decisions that will bring value to many lives and glorify Him? True fulfilment is when we are able to effectively balance all of our roles and understand their connection to our life's mission. It is God's wisdom that guides us to make correct and timely decisions.

I recall that happening on March 6, 2020, at our New York Women Leaders meeting. I always learn so much from these amazing leaders and I am always happy to contribute. I particularly remember giving advice on the necessity of having a Strengths, Weaknesses, Opportunities, Threats (SWOT) analysis for our team. I mentioned the Coronavirus as a threat, although from a strategist viewpoint, more research was required for full confirmation. Afterward, I was plagued with thoughts of the timing of my contribution. I grappled with the urgency of the matter and wondered if, perhaps, it would have been more practical to mention it at a future meeting some months later. At that time, we did not even have one death from this virus in New York. However, I believe that day, was more than my strategy expertise in operation.

That was the day when I dared to present what I felt in my spirit, although it seemed quite farfetched and non-urgent.

Within a week, much faster than any of us could have ever imagined, everything emerged. Our women's conference, scheduled for the week after our meeting, had to be suddenly canceled the day before the event, leaving hundreds of women disappointed and in disbelief. Subsequently, all of the New York conferences were canceled, which impacted all the leaders who were at that meeting the prior week. Within two weeks, the unheard-of happened. Schools, churches – organizations - borders were all closed. The country was on lockdown, followed by the world on lockdown. COVID-19 became a global threat with millions affected worldwide. In just a little over a year, from zero deaths to 53,000 deaths in New York; over 600,000 deaths in USA; 3.9 million deaths globally and over 178 million reported cases of the virus worldwide. Our world is forever changed! My world – my mission is even more engaged!

If God has given you a seat at the table, be obedient to His guidance. Your position at that organization, in that school, community or family is not accidental. God has specifically placed you there with a time-stamped purpose for His glory. Just have faith, lean into God's wisdom, be courageous and speak up, regardless of how outlandish it sounds. God's ways are not man's ways - believe Him!

God may be speaking to you right now, but you are too afraid or too proud to follow. He has sent you many signs and confirmations, but it all seems too illogical, or not packaged the way you envisioned it. If only you would push aside apprehension and believe Him, you would save a lot of wasted time, effort, and resources. The world is awaiting your value. Do not let fear suppress you. Step out in faith and align with God before that season is over.

When we respond to God's nudging, it builds our faith and the faith of others. Numbers 23:19 declares that "God is not a man that He could lie (NKJV)." The beauty about God's direction is, it needs no justification. God can handle that for Himself. We are only responsible for our position of obedience; God is responsible for the outcome. He will bring the validation in due time.

When we do not obey God's voice, we walk in the exhaustion that fear brings. How many times have we found ourselves overthinking or overworking, only to discover that it was all unnecessary when we see how God worked it all out? It does not mean that we become lazy and not put in the required work where necessary, but total self-reliance where we fail to acknowledge God becomes the transgression of pride. Many times, God is just asking us to position ourselves with Him and quit trying to overwhelm ourselves in our own strength. When He demonstrates His power, especially in those back-against-the-wall battles, He is the only One who could get the glory.

2 Chronicles 20:17 gives a powerful example of how God helps us: "You will not need to fight this battle. Position yourselves, stand still and see the salvation of the Lord, who is with you, Oh Judah and Jerusalem. Do not fear or be dismayed; tomorrow go out against them, for the Lord is with you (NKJV)." Yes, our God is willing and ready to fight for us. You could personalize this scripture and insert your name where it says "Judah and Jerusalem." I declare it over myself, "Oh Rhonda – DO NOT FEAR or be intimidated ..." You declare it over yourself: "Oh (YOUR NAME) – DO NOT FEAR or be downcast ..." It is important to note, they still got dressed for battle and went out, but God is the One who brought the victory. As we get dressed and go out daily, let us be aware that God is the One who is gracing us with strength and ability to succeed. Acknowledge Him!

The bible is replete with "fear-not" because it is not God's intention for His children to live in fear, yet many are paralyzed by it. He is constantly speaking over us Isaiah 41.10, "Fear not, for I am with you; be not dismayed for I am your God. I will strengthen you, yes I will help you, I will uphold you with my righteous right hand (NKJV)." He is frequently reminding us that we could rely on His power. How Encouraging!

The important question is, how do we remain calm and stay in faith when faced with the anxieties of life? Well, the profound, yet most basic answer is, to remain in God's love, which He offers to everyone freely. It is up to us to accept it. Prayer, worship, and praises to God are some key ways to express and keep our love connection with Him. It is the beautiful communion; where we get to talk to Him and He communicates back to us. That love connection is our source of peace. Philippians 4:6-7 explains it well, "Be anxious for nothing, but in everything by prayer and supplication, with thanksgiving, let your requests be made known to God; and the peace of God, which surpasses all understanding, will guard your hearts and minds through Christ Jesus (NKJV)."

Yes, God's love is the most powerful antidote for fear. We see it so distinctly in 1 John 4:18-19 "there is no fear in love, but perfect _love casts out fear_ because fear involves torment, ... he who fears, has not been made perfect in love. We love Him because He first loved us (NKJV)." Our daily commitment should be to remain in His love and, seek a willing heart that aligns with His purpose. Why?

Well, simply because Romans 8:28, tells us that, "ALL things work together for GOOD to those who LOVE the Lord and are called according to His purpose (NKJV)." All things! That is the good, the bad, and everything in between. So even if circumstances do not appear so wholesome right now, if you love the Lord and you are in His plan, it is just a matter of time before the benefit of it all is revealed. We see it in the story of Joseph in the Bible. God placed a dream in Him for great leadership, but many times he found himself in dark places because of the evil done to him by others. It still did not prohibit the dream God placed in him from coming to pass. The same will happen for you. Do not abandon your dream because of some uncomfortable detours in your journey – you are only passing through that dark place.

Walking in love sometimes takes extra effort. We could all agree that it could be challenging to love the unlovely; especially those who are intent on hurting us. We need faith to surrender our hurts to the Lord and pray for the offenders. It is so painful to watch the avoidable trouble people create for themselves when they try to hurt God's people. Our response is to ask for God's mercy for them. Jesus said it best on the cross when He uttered, "Father, forgive them for they do not know what they do."

I will not make light of the pain people go through. Indeed, God knows every pain we feel. He does not turn a blind eye when we go through hurts – when we are being treated unfairly. Hebrews 4:15 explains how He feels and understands our pain. We read in Acts 9, where light from heaven struck down Saul on the road to Damascus, on his way to harm God's people. God accosted Him with a piercing question, "Saul, Saul, why are you persecuting ME?" It is very important to note that He did not say, why are you persecuting my children – He made it clear that He (GOD) was the One who was being hurt. This proves that He is in touch with our suffering and He will take care of the situation. In Saul's case, he was converted from his life of wrongdoing to becoming Apostle Paul who wrote so many books in the Bible that blesses us. God came down and handled that situation Himself. That evil was transformed for good.

We get to see the supernatural at work when we are faithful in being the hands, feet, or voice of Jesus, in whatever line of work. God will not call us to do His work, then abandon us when the pressure hits. He fights for us all the way – in our personal lives, in our professional lives, and in ministry.

The love of God in our lives is threatened when we hold onto offenses, and the adversary knows those areas of vulnerability. That is why we need to stay vigilant against hoarding hurts that could lead to bitterness. This is a key area in our lives where all of us will be heavily tested. We are particularly warned of the dangers of the root of bitterness in Hebrews 12:15. It grows into a stubborn tree that could destroy us and others and block our blessing.

Blatant offenses are possibly easier to recognize and address, but we have to be attentive to the subtle ones and submit those too to the Lord. I remember a subtle offense that really affected me. I disliked when people pointed out that I had no children. Although, in their defense, most of them probably were unaware of the struggles I faced. I particularly remember an incident where a church usher greeted me one Mother's Day with "sorry sis, these corsages are only for mothers, not wives without children." It was a straightforward statement, but it was another hit in a vulnerable spot for me. It was over six years of not having children, pangs of miscarriage, and the enemy tried to capitalize on my vulnerability. Whether this woman intended to offend me or not, was not the issue. Whether it is deemed petty or not, was not the issue. Everyone's journey is different, and yes, our feelings should be validated. However, we cannot continue to make that an excuse to remain stuck in defeat; wallow in distress and further damage relationships.

The real issue is, we all need to hold ourselves accountable for our actions. We cannot control the behavior of others or blame others for our reactions, the responsibility is ours to own. Romans 14:12 says that "each of us shall give an account of himself to God NKJV."

Therefore, our primary focus has to be inward. If only we all made self-reflection and self-improvement a priority there would certainly be less conflict. The enemy enjoys us being over-occupied with the wrongdoings of others because it gives us less time to develop ourselves; it depresses us; stagnates us; and it destroys our connections.

The movement of faith requires us to be intentional in rising above our doubts and hurts. We need to surrender it all to God, knowing whatever valley is destined for our journey, God gives us the grace to go through it, as He did for Job. However, we should not be comfortable in situations where He only intended for us to pass through. We need to know when that season is over, let it go, and allow God's love, forgiveness, and plan to prevail.

It is true that some hurts may take longer than others to overcome, but God is faithful to bring purpose out of our pain if we dare to believe and relinquish it all to Him. Healing often follows our surrender to His plan. I have seen that happen so many times in my life. For example, my response to that usher's comment was, to ignore it, refocus and press through in worship and praises to God and enjoy the church service. That decision led me to a remarkable encounter with the Lord. I believe a breakthrough happened that day, because approximately NINE MONTHS after that incident, I was holding my miracle – my firstborn son, after seven years of marriage – the very thing the experts said would not happen. I shared more details of this story in another book that I compiled: *"Empowered to Overcome Tough Seasons of Life."*

Could it be that you are about to receive your blessing, that is why the offenses are intensified? Could it be that you are heading for a breakthrough, that is why it seems as if all hell has broken loose against you or your family? Maybe your miracle is already here and the discouragement, hurt – darkness you are experiencing, are distractions to prevent you from stepping into that reality.

I admonish you to ignore the distractions, push through and focus on your blessing ahead! That is exactly what Jesus demonstrated to us in the way he handled the offenses, even from those who were close to Him. We see it clearly with Peter who disowned Him; Thomas who doubted Him and Judas who betrayed Him. He made a lot of valuable investments in their lives

— His time, His teachings — His resources — His Love. Yet they panicked and turned away from Him when fear struck. Peter was afraid to be identified with Jesus; he retreated into blending in with the crowd. Thomas feared that Jesus had completely abandoned them; he forgot about the miracles - the supernatural - and fell back into relying solely on his natural senses — seeing and touching. Judas feared that Lord was not the all-sufficient connection — Jireh (Provider); he digressed into betraying the Lord to fill his money bag. Jesus' purpose was still on track; He was still on the way to the cross then to glory and He was not surprised by any of it. He knew exactly what they would do. As a matter of fact, He confronted them on those issues and offered His love and forgiveness. Sadly, only Peter and Thomas embraced that restoration.

How do we handle people who hurt us, especially those who were once close to us — perhaps those whom we have helped? Regardless of their motives, whether for fame — recognition with certain groups; fortune — for money, materialism; or due to misjudgment, jealousy, or otherwise - how do we handle people who are intent on being our enemies - those who become agents of darkness and are filled with hatred of our light? Again, we have to surrender them all to Jesus and take that courageous step of faith where Jesus tells us to still show God's love and pray for them. This is one of the hardest tests of life, but to grow in our faith, we all must walk this difficult journey. Walking in love is an intentional decision and step of faith. To do otherwise is too burdensome. Dr. Martin Luther King, Jr. says it well "I have decided to stick with love. Hate is too great a burden to bear." In Matthew 5:38-48, we see the nature of God where He shows us how He allows everyone, whether good or evil, to benefit from the sun and the rain. One of the thought-provoking questions in this passage is, where He questions us about what is so special about loving those who love us? That is the easiest thing to do; anybody could do that, whether a believer in Christ or not.

To love God's way requires His strength; it is totally impossible to do it on our own. When our hearts are willing to obey His approach, He somehow finds a way to fashion it all together to develop us – to advance us to the next level. The hard truth is we have to go through that process of offering love and forgiveness to everyone as Jesus did, but it will not always result in the reconnection of all relationships. God is the One who determines whom we should restore and whom we should release. When we are too proud to reconnect with the people He wants in our lives, we have no peace! When we hold onto the people whose season is up in our lives, we have no peace!

Yes, our journey does not consist of only mountaintop experiences; valley seasons are inevitable but He promises to be with us always. It seemed like a week did not go by since the Spring of 2020, where we did not say "our condolences and prayers" to someone. The fear of death hung over the nations. The reality is many of us lost loved ones and everyday people are still grieving loss and facing the threat of death. Yet the Lord promises to be with us in those difficult times. The psalmist gives the comforting reminder in Psalm 23:4 that "...though I walk through the valley of the shadow of death, I will fear no evil, for You are with me (NKJV)".

We have the assurance that when we go through tough seasons, that same "Fourth Man in the Fire", who was with the three Hebrew young men in the Bible, is also in the heat of the battle with us. We trust Him and the process. His presence comforts us, silences fear, and gives eternal hope to those who believe in Him.

Every experience, good and bad, prepares us for ministry. In my situation, I am drawn to prayer for women, especially those who are experiencing struggles like mine. As a couple, my husband and I are burdened to pray for people in dead-end situations like the ones we experienced. Many times, God answers with miracles, either by turning the situation around or by giving His peace for the journey. For instance, we saw that turnaround a few years ago when we were invited to minister in New York. After preaching, the Lord led my husband to single out just one woman in the congregation for prayer. Her husband joined us in prayer at the altar. My husband then declared that her miracle will happen in the new year. Within just a little over nine months, God blessed them with a beautiful baby girl. Unknown to us, they were believing God for this to happen for a number of years. God turned their situation around instantly. All Glory to the Lord! In other situations, God has helped others to find peace and fulfillment in fostering or nurturing through teaching and various ways of sharing His love. Our pain over the years turned into purpose!! The same is happening for you right now. Purpose is evolving. That painful situation you are going through will make you an effective minister, if you dare to yield to God's plan.

Remember, your ministry is not just from the pulpit, it could be anywhere and in practical ways. For example, when someone starts a new role, recall your struggles when you were new in that position and help them to acclimate. If you know of resources that could help someone lead a better life, share that information with them. To allow others to struggle when we have an answer is selfish and a missed opportunity to show love. There is one practice I have always maintained over the years at every place where I worked, whether secularly or in ministry. Whenever I moved on from a role, I always left guidelines for the person that will fill that role. It reduces the anxieties of that person and is a very simple way to show love – to show God's love. It makes your light stand out in the darkness. Many times, there may be fear of losing something in sharing knowledge, but your light does not become dimmer or lose value when you share it with others. Remember, what God has for you, no man can take it away. Sometimes we miss our opportunity of sowing into others because we fear rejection. We cannot force anyone to accept our love, we could only offer it.

So, let us pray against the spirit of fear and advance in our assignment with God's help, like David, the shepherd boy, in the Bible, who fearlessly defeated the giant which caused an army of strong men to shrink. You are not too young in age or too inexperienced with God, to march forward in faith and defeat your giants. Keep your eyes on the light ahead and take those bold steps, even if you feel wobbly at times like toddlers taking those first steps – even if you experience missteps, trips, and falls. Just keep getting up and moving forward. You will get there if you keep stepping out and keep trying. What would have happened if we had abandoned our attempt at walking during the toddler stage because of some missteps or fear of walking? Our world would have been crippled.

The same will happen if you do not take those faith steps. There is a unique God-given mission attached to you that will be crippled if you do not step out in faith.

Reflecting on children and their fearlessness reminds me of one winter when my husband and I were headed home. Our car suddenly slid downhill and spun out of control into oncoming traffic. Horrified, as other vehicles were also spinning around us; we quickly looked toward the back seat to make sure that our five-year-old son was okay. To our amazement, he had a big grin on his face; eyes wide open with excitement, as he exclaimed, "Whoa! That was fun! DO IT AGAIN, DADDY!"

His unexpected reaction brought some humor to a scary situation and helped to calm us, much to the surprise of onlookers. Oh, the faith of children! It is no wonder Jesus tells us in Matthew 18:1-4, that in order to enter His Kingdom, we need to become like them. Their humility, faith, and trust lead to their carefree and fearless nature. After all, someone capable has it all under control.

With every miracle the Lord performs; our faith is strengthened for the next step. We are encouraged for the next battle. Therefore, our response to every seemingly fearful situation should be one of great expectation, where we too like children, get to say with resilient faith to our Father in Heaven, just "DO, IT AGAIN, DADDY!"

Questions for Reflection

1. Do you feel your faith has been crippled by fear?

2. Do you believe the Lord can help you overcome fear?

3. Are there limitations that you would like to break from your life?

4. Are there offenses that you are hoarding?

5. Is there a miracle you need?

Let us Pray

Heavenly Father, we come before Your throne of grace, believing that You can remove any pain, hurt, care – offense that has been plaguing us. We ask for Your love; which casts out all fear, to overflow in our lives. Give us the strength to forgive those who have hurt us and draw them to Your love. We pray that you help us to boldly step out in faith and become whatever you have designed for us to be. We ask that you remove anything that is not attached to our assignment and bring only what is part of your divine plan for us. We pray in the Name of Jesus, Amen!

Affirmations

- My faith is in God

- God is guiding me

- I am courageous

- I am motivated to step out

- I release offenses

- I embrace God's love

- I am making good choices

- I face and overcome my fears with God's help

- I am seeing opportunities

- I believe God's report

- I am stepping out in faith and over fear

- I DARE TO BELIEVE!

Helpful Scriptures

- 1 John 4:18

- Isaiah 41:10

- 2 Timothy 1:7

- 1 John 4:18

- Psalm 56:3-4

- Ezekiel 33:26

- Joshua 1:9

My Faith Steps

_____

_____

_____

_____

_____

_____

_____

_____

_____

_____

CHAPTER 2

Author Carol L. Brown

Birthing Faith

Author Carol L. Brown

After four years of marriage, we were excited to learn that we were expecting our first baby. We went through the initial doctor's appointments and the first sonogram. We were overjoyed about our blessing to come. At about twelve weeks; following a glorious weekend of sharing our news, we received a call from our doctor that Monday. He stated he wanted us to have a good weekend so waited until afterwards to call. He went further, stating that there was a concern with the baby's anatomy and that he wanted to send me to a team of specialists for a higher-level sonogram and he also informed me that the specialists would handle my care for the duration of the pregnancy.

We were confused and concerned at what he meant regarding the baby's "anatomy." We were directed to a team of specialists for high-risk pregnancies at a hospital about forty-five minutes away. This information left us wondering and confused; but we remained prayerful and went for the appointment.

It was explained that our baby's condition was Anencephaly or an anencephalic pregnancy. This is a neural tube birth defect. This is where a baby is born with an underdeveloped brain and an

31

incomplete skull. Anencephaly is a defect in the formation of a baby's neural tube during development. A baby born with anencephaly might be stillborn or survive only a few hours to a few days after birth as there is no cure for anencephaly.

It was also explained that there is an increased medical risk involved with the mother carrying a fetus with anencephaly. I was told the mother usually carries more amniotic fluid which could cause the uterus to stretch larger with the potential to detach from the body, and the mother could hemorrhage; even to death. Parents may be offered the opportunity to terminate, which is exactly what they encouraged us to do.

We left that appointment with so much information to process and our excitement turned into a fight of sorts. As a believer in Jesus, devastating news is an opportunity to 'go to war' as one seeks the Lord; prays and goes to war spiritually for the victory and promises of the Lord in our lives. That was exactly what we were preparing to do.

One thing I knew was that terminating the pregnancy was not an option. Though given the medical facts, I was courageous enough to believe in a miracle from our Lord Jesus. I thought perhaps He would heal my baby and that we would have a testimony of this miracle performed by the hand of the Lord. Although thoughtful of the road ahead, I was secure in what I knew was the Lord's plan. I was concerned, but I believed that the Lord had a plan to perform a miracle, and that work would ultimately draw others to Him.

We went through the following months of having to continue our visits with the specialized unit and team of doctors. At times, we would feel pressured to terminate the pregnancy during these appointments. I had a doctor ask me, "what do you think is going to happen?" I explained that "I am believing in God for a miracle and if not, He would prepare us for what's to come." He further explained that he and the team would rather my body not go through the possible complications of the delivery since the baby; according to them, would not survive. We remained firm in our decision not to terminate!

The next few months I was determined to enjoy my first pregnancy. It is always nice to know someone else who is pregnant at the same time and I had two ladies I knew from church, who were also expecting. Not only were we pregnant at the same time, but were due in the same month. There was a bit of a 'baby boom' happening at our church. Some members knew of our pregnancy diagnosis and joined us in prayer and belief for God to perform a miracle. As the months progressed, all was well with me carrying the baby. I did carry larger, which was what the doctors stated could happen, due to increased amniotic fluid, and not related to the baby's actual size.

Friends, family and church family threw us a baby shower. Now this may sound strange, but we believed the Lord would perform a miracle. We had that kind of faith to believe He would turn this around. As the weeks continued to pass by, the team of doctors met with us to discuss the delivery. Given the prognosis, they thought it was better for me not to give birth via cesarean section, to avoid the surgery and possible medical repercussions. With natural births, it is the baby's skull and head that guides the baby down the birth canal to be born. Without a full skull, the baby would have to be pushed more by the face, since that structure is the same. They also did want me to carry up until the very end; still raising fear of increased amniotic fluid and chances of hemorrhaging.

At eight months I was experiencing discomfort. I went to the doctor and they immediately had me admitted into the hospital because I had a leak of amniotic fluid. I prayed that I would deliver naturally and go into labor on my own. During that stay, I experienced increased discomfort and started to have contractions.

My husband started to make his way to the hospital. It looked like that would be the day. The contractions and pain increased, and the medical team started to prepare me for delivery. The pain further increased and they gave me Demerol, a pain medication, intravenously.

The pain medication would cause me to sleep even in between contractions, but I would wake up or be more alert during the discomfort of the contractions. My loving husband was there by my side. When it was time, I was instructed to push. It was quite hard and took a while and a lot of pushing and maneuvering by doctors, but finally this awaited moment was here. Our baby was born! It's a girl! The team tended to her and wrapped her nicely before I saw and held her.

Only weighing just over four pounds, she was beautiful! To my devastation, she did have the condition the doctors stated. Looking at her, she was beautiful and whole. There was a thick crocheted hat on her head so we could not see the skull but her face, arms, hands, were perfect! She began to turn blue. Even in that moment, I was not giving up! My mother-in-law and sister-in-law who I knew were women of faith were there with us. I asked where was my brother-in-law, who was also my pastor. I figured if we were unable, he could pray one last prayer for a miracle. When my brother-in-law and pastor arrived; he prayed along with us for our baby!

Have you ever been given something that you thought was yours to keep, but it did not last? Well, that was our outcome. Our baby was not ours to keep. Sad and devastated, we clung to those precious moments we had with her, hugging and kissing her, realizing she would not be coming home with us. We named our baby girl Faith! Faith was a girl name we had already picked out although we were not sure if we were having a boy or a girl. It was always my dream to have a girl and name her Faith. There was that thought that if I give her this name, maybe I would not have a daughter to call by that name around the house one day. Well, we did give her my dream name, FAITH!

The hospital was certain to place mothers who experienced this type of outcome in a location away from mothers celebrating the birth of babies and also away from the nursery. I was placed on a floor and room where women were recuperating from other GYN issues and surgeries. I laid in that hospital bed that night crying. Although sad, I had peace and slept so soundly, like a baby, that night. I knew that the road ahead to heal would not be enjoyable, BUT I HAD PEACE! I saw this through and did as my convictions *led* me. I realize that many circumstances may lead to a woman terminating a pregnancy. I have also heard from some of them personally, where they would be calculating the age of the child and constantly wondering what would have happened if they had kept the baby. I had peace knowing that I saw this through, even though I believed for a different outcome. Quite frankly I KNEW our baby would live! I had more of a tug-of-war going on with my Lord, questioning this outcome … BUT PEACE! Although the outcome may not be what you were hoping for, if you are obedient to what God is saying, He gives you peace beyond your own understanding. You may go after something God told you to do without the expected outcome, but God's peace is priceless.

We left the hospital a day or so after and headed home. Family members were sure to lovingly remove all baby gifts and items out of our sight. I learned through this experience that I, and many, do not mind the reminders and talking about it. One may want the memory of their loved one to live, and not be so quick to rush their memories away. I also learned that telling a woman, "you can have another…" is also *not* helpful. It is like rushing the removal of the precious life that mother just held. I later had a family member confess that they read an article of how to handle someone who went through this type of loss and apologized for how they removed all items and handled this situation from the beginning. Well, you do not know until you experience it, but a good rule is to take the time to do some research if you are dealing with an unfamiliar area in supporting someone.

We had a small funeral and burial for our baby girl. The casket remained closed and we did not have her prepared for viewing, but held on to the precious time we shared with her after her birth. The hospital also gave us a keepsake box with her picture, a snippet of her hair, the garments they placed on her, and other small sentimental items, which were all very precious. The song that I requested to be sung was "I Surrender All." Clearly, I had to surrender this loss to the Lord. One may say, "well you knew the diagnosis." I tell you; my faith was stronger and I believed for a different outcome. I knew Him to be a God of miracles.

Family and friends gave us a week away by the water, but we were still close to where we lived. We had precious time to cry, talk, pray and *begin* to heal. At this place there was a spa where they had arranged a facial for me. I laid there having my face treated and steamed. Next the esthetician began placing warm strips of cloth to further the treatment over my face. In that moment, I began to hyperventilate and I had to snatch them off. To my surprise, I thought of my baby in a casket with that covering over her unable to breathe. The feeling surprised me, but it was very real. I experienced this again, months later at a women's retreat, where I was sleeping in the lower bunk bed. The top bunk bed over me gave me the same feeling, and I had to get up and sleep on the sofa. Again, the thought of my baby being covered in a casket troubled me.

Over the next weeks, we returned to our normal daily activities and work. I had many conversations with the Lord. I was believing God for a miracle and He did perform one. He clearly told me "YOU ARE THE MIRACLE!" He reminded me how he kept me through this experience and how I did not have to suffer the possible dangerous side effects. Although I had to deal with challenging days and special days like Mother's Day and Father's Day; there were times when I went home and cried. God strengthened me to handle those situations. I was able to face friends and others I encountered who had their precious babies and I was able to celebrate with them! The Lord filled me with hope that one day I too would bring a baby home to raise. I found comfort in this scripture: "The Lord is near to the brokenhearted and saves those who are crushed in spirit." (Psalm 34:18 NKJV).

As time went by, my husband and I began genetic counseling. There was nothing in our family and medical histories, that would have given us or doctors a clue as to why this happened. We understood that we had a higher risk of experiencing another neural tube birth defect if we had another baby. I was placed on high doses of folic acid. Once again, it was time to step out in Faith!

*****

Two years later; within the same month, we gave birth to a healthy baby girl; with two more healthy girls to follow. We are blessed now to have three daughters to raise; with our first born in Heaven. The miracles of the Lord continue to evolve in ministry.

Have you ever gone through a devastating experience that has equipped you to minister to others? That is exactly what I am continuously seeing. The resulting compassion for effective teaching in ministry is remarkable. There was one instance with a lady at our church, who came out of the hospital after experiencing a miscarriage. I was surprised that she specifically asked my pastors to speak with me. I met with her, and although we did not discuss a lot of the details, I realized that she knew I *understood* her pain. I was able to encourage and uplift her through her difficult time.

Having faith was not the end of my story and it was not over that day! God had and still has a plan to take us through and use all things together for our good. Romans 8:28 "And we know that all things work together for good to those who love the God, to those who are the called according to His purpose NKJV."

There is a special writing that was written by a dear friend, Pastor Shawna Hagans. It is displayed in our home and it still blesses us to this day. I would like to share with you:

From the Lord:

Why Faith?

Why Faith, Lord? Why did we conceive Faith? Why did we have Faith? Why did you allow her to grow and move in us only to allow the enemy to take away the substance of the things we hoped for and the evidence of the things we did not see?

My son, my daughter, if you did not conceive her in your belly, if you did not allow Faith to grow and move in you, she would not be substance, she would not exist. But because you conceived her in your belly and allowed her to grow and move in you, a new life now exists that would not have existed otherwise. Now, Faith IS the substance of things hoped for and the evidence of things not seen to everyone else.

And think not that the enemy has stolen anything from you. For Faith was fearfully and wonderfully made in you for one Purpose: That I might know her. That I might hold her in my arms. For I could only choose special people like you to have Faith for Me. For I chose faith from the foundation of the world to go from glory to glory. From the glory of a carefree existence in your womb to the glory of a carefree existence FOREVER in my presence.

For without Faith, it is impossible to please God. My son and my daughter, THANK YOU FOR HAVING FAITH. FOR I AM WELL PLEASED!

From Faith:

Have Faith

One day my sweet Jesus whispered to my parents' heart and said: "Bob and Carol have Faith."

My parents received His words with joy and said: "Let's have Faith." When I was conceived, I was as small as a grain of a mustard seed, but I grew. I lived and moved and had my being in the womb of my mother Carol. And when the doctors had given up hope and didn't believe or understand why my parents continued to hold onto me, they said: "Don't have Faith."

But my parents chose to listen to Jesus and not to the doctors. And when I was born, they looked at me as I rested in their arms with thankfulness and said: "We had Faith." I am the substance of what they hoped for and the evidence of the things unseen by many; I am Faith. Faith Brown.

As they held me, unknown to them, Jesus stood nearby watching and waiting to hold me too; yearning to take me into His bosom. He whispered to my parents and said: "Without Faith it is impossible to please Me." So, as my parents wept, I closed my eyes and woke up in His arms. He looked at them and said:

"THANK YOU FOR HAVING FAITH"

So, if you are ever believing the Father for anything, remember me,

FAITH BROWN

That beautiful writing above sent from the Lord, to us, truly communicates how Faith was birthed in us and reminds us to have faith even in tough times!

So many times, we go through situations in life that seem unfair. Maybe you feel stuck over something that did not go according to your plan? Have you had something that you thought was yours to keep; perhaps a marriage, relationship, job, health, etc., but it is gone? Do not give up and do not lose hope. Your story is not over. God has a bigger plan. Dare to Believe in Him! When reality and faith collide, allow faith to prevail!

Questions for Reflection

1. Have you ever done, what you felt was the right thing to do, but the outcome did not go according to your plan?

2. Have you held a blessing you thought was yours to keep and had to watch it slip away from you?

3. Are you personally in need of healing regarding a heartbreaking situation?

4. What has a difficult situation taught you?

5. Do you believe that even in your disappointment that God could work it out for good?

Let us Pray

Lord, I surrender my hurts and disappointments to You. I lean on You to heal my broken heart and take me through this difficult time. Help me not to blame You for any outcome that I did not expect, and to trust that You have a greater purpose. Help me not to compare myself with others or question why their prayers were answered and mine overlooked. I depend on You to uphold me while I purposely choose to expand my faith!

Affirmations

- I am at peace

- I trust God

- I am brave

- I am surrendered to God

- I accept God's plan

- My story is not over

- I DARE TO BELIEVE!

Helpful Scriptures

- Hebrews 11:1

- 2 Corinthians 12:10

- Colossians 2:6-7

- John 16:33

My Faith Steps

_____

_____

_____

_____

_____

_____

_____

_____

_____

_____

CHAPTER 3

Author JoAnne Eronini

Making it Through

Author JoAnne Eronini

On a clear evening in late October, I experienced something that changed my life. Though I am originally from Virginia; I now reside in Staten Island, New York. Using public transportation to get to and from Staten Island can be a bit challenging. If you miss a scheduled ferry in the evenings, you must wait for thirty minutes in order to catch the next ferry. After working all day and then attending an evening class, I was more than ready to get home to my family. I saw the last ferry door closing and I sprinted like crazy – with several bags in tow. Of course, few females travel throughout New York; especially during the workday, without a bag or two to carry the items we tend to pick up between our daily travels. Needless to say, I barely managed to dash through the closing doors; giving a smile of thanks to the ferry staff for allowing me to squeeze through.

As I walked along the plank to enter the ferry, I attempted to catch my breath and slow my pace. That is when it hit me like a ton of bricks! I began to feel an explosion in my head. 'Ba-boom, ba-boom, ba-boom' the pressure pounded in my head. Every step was excruciatingly painful. I could barely hold the two bags that I had carried onto the ferry and my legs were starting to succumb to what felt like a partial paralysis. Of course, pride and grace are everything – so I managed to hold myself up and shuffled along to find an empty seat.

Once seated I shifted uncontrollably as my mind was all over the place. I did not want to be a sick passenger on the ferry and hold up the other passengers who were trying to get home on time. I did not want to bring attention to myself, so I struggled to keep it together, but could not find a comfortable position to ease the pain. I just wanted to get home to my family. I thought to myself– "this too shall pass". However, it was not passing fast enough for me. Despite the agonizing pain, I managed to exit the ferry and make it to the bus stop, but cannot tell you how I made it there.

Have any of you ever experienced a pain so unbearable that you lacked clarity. That was the kind of pain I was feeling. As I boarded the bus, I was praying that a seat would be available. I paid my fare; and found an empty seat. I am not sure how long it took me to arrive to my stop, but it seemed like the longest ride ever. I managed to exit the bus at my stop, and walk the two blocks to my house. As usual I called my husband on the way to alert him that I would be arriving soon, but I did not share my ordeal on the ferry with him because I did not want him to worry.

My prayers were answered. I made it home safely and was then able to 'collapse' with a sigh of relief to be there. I gently closed the door; greeted my husband and told him of my situation. My husband gave me some over-the-counter medication, hoping it would relieve the pain. The pain did not subside, rather it intensified. So, my husband took me to the Emergency Room (ER). While at the ER, I received medication to lower my extremely elevated blood pressure. However, this still did not relieve the pain that I was experiencing in my head. The day after was also no better. I was able to get an emergency appointment with my newly selected primary care physician and after listening to my concerns, he ordered a Computerized Axial Tomography (CAT) scan. Though this was my very first visit with my primary care physician, I felt comfortable with him and appreciated the level of his care. At this point, I believed that our supplication was heard. I thanked God that we were able to schedule a CAT scan for the following Monday morning. Throughout the weekend I remained calm; to not elevate the pain in my head.

*****

Decision day! Monday arrived and after the morning devotions with my husband, we headed out for my scheduled CAT scan.

Though I was still feeling pain, my husband and I decided to make a few stops before heading back home, following the scheduled scan. Shortly after returning to the car from our first stop, I received a phone call from my primary care physician. Immediately after his greeting, he informed me that he had the results from the CAT scan, that I had taken earlier that day. He informed me that it was determined that I had bilateral bleeding on my brain as well as fluid on the brain. He instructed me to go to the ER immediately and then the call dropped.

Stunned by the news, I was asking myself, 'did I just hear that correctly?' In shock, I repeated what the doctor said, to my husband. As he continued to drive the car, I tried to contact the doctor to reaffirm what he had just told me so that my husband could hear it as well; to no avail. With no luck of reconnecting with my doctor, we followed his instructions and headed to the ER.

Once at the ER, we registered and explained the situation that brought me there. After a brief waiting period, I met with the Triage Nurse to again explain my situation. The nurse appeared to be calm, but I could sense a bit of urgency in her actions after she heard my story. Within minutes I was taken to the ER examination area. While on the gurney, a multitude of staff came to my side to perform a battery of tests. As I laid there, I prayed with assurance that my God would never leave me nor forsake me. Personalizing 1 Pet 2:24 to my situation, declaring, "By His stripes [I] am Healed." I repeated my favorite scripture; Jeremiah 29:11, "I know the plans I have for you…". The hospital staff were able to consult with my primary care physician and learned of his diagnosis. After reviewing their own exams which included another CAT scan, they confirmed the diagnosis of bilateral bleeding on the brain along with fluid on the brain.

In a matter of minutes, I was taken to the Intensive Care Unit (ICU). I continued to remain calm and I continued to praise God. You can say that I had a peace over me that surpassed all of my own understanding. I had bleeding and fluid on my brain and all I could do was praise God and thank Him for my life. As I laid in the hospital bed, in the ICU unit, feeling like a pin cushion from all the needle sticks, I continued to smile and praise God because I knew that He would never leave me.

Have you experienced life challenges that weighed you down and tried to get the best of you? You may find yourself not knowing how you would find the strength to make it through? Dare to believe like the woman with the issue of blood in Bible, whose strong faith and desire for healing led her to say, "if I can just touch the hem of His garment, I would be made whole." I encourage you to stand on your faith. Although that faith may be as small as a mustard seed, it will get you through.

Today, as I go deeper into studying the word of God, I now have a better understanding of what Satan wanted – for me to experience the spirit of Amalek (Exodus 17:8-16) where the sole purpose is to break down and destroy the faith of people in God. This happens by making us cast doubt on God. John 10:10 NKJV says "The thief does not come except to steal, and to kill, and to destroy. I am come that they may have life, and that they may have it more abundantly." So, because I built a place in my heart, I was not going to allow myself to sink down and doubt the word of God. I knew this for sure, I am fearfully and wonderfully made and I was not going to have the spirit of fear. I was going to continue to believe that my God would answer my prayers with the same assurance and the comfort that God would never leave me nor forsake me. I felt stronger than ever that there was still more for me to do.

The following evening, I was prepped for a procedure that would take place on day two of my hospital stay. With a few minor interruptions the procedure continued as scheduled. No, it was not brain surgery but an *angiogram*, which is a diagnostic test that uses x-rays to take pictures of your blood vessels. A long flexible catheter is inserted into the blood stream to deliver dye- a contrast agent, into the arteries making them visible on the x-ray. A small cut is then made in the skin over one of the arteries, usually near the groin or wrist and a local anesthetic is used.

Still with no fear or anxiety, I quietly reflected on the words from Psalm 91, "…He who dwells in the secret place the Most High shall abide under the shadow of the Almighty. … He is my refuge and my fortress, my God, in Him will I trust…. (NKJV)". The procedure was completed, and all went well. Life challenges could cause anyone to be flustered, but with God by my side, I had the power over fear. Following the procedure, I was informed that I may have a small amount of discomfort at the site of the wound, but I felt nothing. That was an affirmation for me. God was in control, Amen! As I continued to rest and praise the Mighty Name of God, the intensity of the headaches began to decrease. With less intense headaches I was able to increase the length of my conversations and found myself witnessing to the hospital staff about the goodness of His glory. At one point I caught myself and cried out to God – how is this possible? I am here in this hospital bed; body bruised from needle sticks and tubes coming from my arms and I have not – not once – stopped praising Your name. When the situation seemed that it would call for brain surgery, it did not happen. When we rest in Him, we can see how He changes the results. Hallelujah! I know that the old me – the one who did not have faith the size of a mustard seed would have been in panic mode. Since I cry at the drop of a hat, I probably would have been in tears every step of the way; but no, not this time. I was now grounded in my faith and in my trust in the Almighty God.

There were things that occurred; days turned into nights, and family from near and far, as well as fellowship partners, came and went. However, the most uncertain thing of it all, which puzzled the doctors, was, what was the cause of this unfortunate thing? Doctors repeatedly would ask, 'did you hit your head on something?' in various ways; inquiring, 'did you fall?' and my response was consistently – 'no'. With no explanation for this medical prognosis and all test results showing no need for brain surgery; the medical team were left bemused.

Signs, wonders and miracles. The CAT scans clearly revealed bleeding on my brain along with fluid on my brain. I said, thank you God for your protection! The angiogram revealed no blocked arteries or leaks. I said thank you God for your deliverance! The spinal tap revealed that the fluid in my cranial area was appropriate. I said, thank you God for your mercy! Three neurosurgeons from the hospital had no answers except to say this will go away. I said;

thank you God for your love! After nine days of being confined to the hospital bed and over $75,000 in medical bills, I was medically cleared by the care team and provided with a discharge date.

My post discharge orders included bedrest and medical follow-up appointments. I walked out of the hospital with no brain surgery; available health insurance, and yes; faith as small as a mustard seed. The medications prescribed were a blood pressure medication and a pain medication in the event I felt discomfort at the wound sites, of which I did not need; and yes, faith as small as a mustard seed.

After a few weeks of bed rest at home we located a neurosurgeon with no affiliation with the hospital for an additional medical opinion. During the initial visit, he requested a copy of all of the hospital records, and he ordered another CAT scan. He too was baffled by the medical experience I shared with him. Bilateral bleeding on the brain; no surgery was needed! Fluid on the brain, and no surgery needed! Angiogram administered; results clear. Spinal tap administered; results clear. The scan that he ordered showed everything clear, no surgery needed. He too was extremely bewildered by the entire ordeal. After several additional follow-up visits to his office, I was released from his care. I said, thank you God that I made it through! That was two years ago.

Today I am a living witness that miracles do happen and that God answers prayers. I have a testimony to share with others. He *has* a plan for my life and He *has* a plan for your life as well. I encourage you to get out of your comfort zone and be a witness. All things are possible when we approach it from a spiritual standpoint. Tell your story of how you made it through whatever troubling time that tried to derail you; that tried to make you doubt your God or second guess your faith. Testify of how you overcame the enemy's plan to steal your joy by walking in resilient faith and trusting in God's word. Boldly dance like David, remembering His goodness and the love He has for you to MAKE IT THROUGH! AMEN!

Questions for Reflection

Are you going through an Amalek moment (low place) in your life?

1. How are you making it through?

2. Do you believe that God can help you make it through?

3. Read about Joshua's Amalek moment in Exodus. How did he make it through?

4. Read about Moses' Amalek moment in Exodus. How did he make it through?

5. Do you believe God could use this situation to help you see His glory?

Let us Pray

Heavenly Father, we praise and glorify Your name. You are our Shield and Buckler; our ever-present help in times of need. We thank you for Your grace and Your mercy. Thank you for always being with us. We understand that when we seek Your Kingdom first, there is a hedge of protection over our lives. I pray Deuteronomy 31:6, over every life "Be strong and courageous, do not be afraid or terrified … for the Lord your God goes with you …", that is, the hospital room; the court room; the board room – everywhere. We believe 2 Chronicles 7:14, that healing and forgiveness is available for us when we call upon Your name and turn from wrong. Thank you, for Your healing power. I believe you will heal our bodies. I pray that we remember that You are our refuge and strength. Lord, bless all those who have read these words and show Your signs, wonders, and miracles in their lives as you did in mine. Amen.

Affirmations

- I am grateful for God's goodness

- God's Hand is on my life

- I lean on God

- I am protected

- I am calm even in chaotic situations

- I am free of worry

- I will make it through every barrier

- I DARE TO BELIEVE

Helpful Scriptures

- Psalm 46:1:

- 2 Thessalonians 3:16:

- Philippians 4:7:

- Psalm 29:11:

My Faith Steps

_____

_____

_____

_____

_____

_____

_____

_____

_____

_____

CHAPTER 4

Author Crystal Lodico

Rahab the Redeemed

Author Crystal Lodico

Becoming a missionary was never something I ever thought about in my early life. Receiving an approved certificate commissioning me into a position of serving others in the name of Jesus has been one of the greatest living moments to date. Although being very confident in the calling God placed over my life, sometimes there is an insecurity in sharing with other missionaries or Christians some true elements of my testimony.

When surrounded by tales of peers who grew up living a devout life for Jesus, I tend to stick to "A woman from the world now called to missions" tagline, usually leaving out details. The path that led me to salvation, was not quite the way most would expect from a person who is allowing God to be the author of her purpose. Even though my parents are Christians, we were not always growing in our faith. My childhood was not going to a Christian Summer camp, singing 'Father Abraham'; I actually attended Vacation Bible School (VBS) once. I did not have a purity ring like all the "good girls" and certainly struggled with self-worth prompting falling into an abusive relationship.

Resilient Faith: Dare to Believe

As a young adult, my college education was not from a 'bible college' studying to become a youth pastor. I had a primary goal of being a boss babe in the media world; a vision that propelled me to attend Hunter College of New York City; completing a degree in Communications and Media. To pay the price tag for living in one of the most vibrant cities of the world, while still having time to hit the books; the best jobs for fast money meant working in club venues. My identity was wrapped in a red dress handing out sparklers to all the fist-pumping big shots who bought a $2,000 bottle of champagne. To add more to the story; at the time, I was living with boyfriends who were not the type of men God intended for me.

Within the eight years of chasing a dream, a lot happened. Yes, before I was not living my God-given purposeful life, but it is beautiful to see how Christ's love is persistent. If you are one of those people who grew up always knowing God and stronger in staying faithful, I am not knocking your testimony; instead, I admire it, and at times, I wished for it for myself. During my breaking points, a common question I would cry out to the Lord is "Why didn't you protect me the way you did for them?" Here is what I have come to learn when dealing with our pasts and our potential futures. God is in control; He is the writer of our life's novel, and if you lean into Him more than any circumstance, He has a significant rewrite up His sleeve.

If one turned back a few pages to the first twenty years of my life, there would probably be suspecting questions on how God could even consider calling a girl who had such a messy history to share the gospel among nations. There are a lot of technicalities that build a testimony; I would be lying if I said everything was a mistake. A lot of the people I meet and have memories with are significant to who I am today. I am not suggesting you live a reckless life because God consistently forgives. While He does forgive if you ask, it is not a 'pass' to continue living out an old narrative in lieu of receiving forgiveness.

I endured a list of consequences giving into fleshly desires; one of them being a feeling of emptiness at the end of each selfish endeavor. Christ is the only one who can erase our errors and give us a fresh beginning. We all have individual stories. One day, if we choose, instead of writing them on our own, we surrender the pen over to Jesus. It is because of Jesus I am made anew; my past is FORGIVEN.

"In whom we have redemption … the forgiveness of sins."

Colossians 1:14 (NKJV)

The Lord guided me to start reading the Bible from the beginning rather than usually jumping around to whichever book feels right. In Joshua; chapter two, there is a woman who also had a past. Her name is Rahab. Her job description: prostitute. With the knowledge of her line of work, she probably was the least qualified person to be used by God. She was living a life that was the result of her choices. One day, the Lord presented her with an opportunity to choose Heaven over Earth.

Joshua sent two spies into the city of Jericho, which was a land promised to Israel. Rahab gave these two men shelter in her home, knowing they were agents of faith, dedicated to the One True God.

"For the Lord your God, He is God in heaven above
and on earth beneath"

Joshua 2:11 (NKJV)

When asked by the King of Jericho to hand them over, she decided to protect their lives and escort them to safety. The two men gave her a scarlet rope to hang over her door, to use as a symbol of protection when Joshua and his army arrived to dethrone the King and claim the city. By her actions, Rahab not only was invited to the kingdom of Israel but then added to the lineage of Jesus Christ. Talk about a plot twist! Rahab was redeemed.

Reading the tale of Rahab and her willingness to serve God despite of her track record, helps to encourage us that the Lord can use anyone for His purpose. It is humbling to me that in every occasion I think how He has transformed my life. In desperation for redemption, the Lord took my submission and began creating a storyline better than I could expect. He is the only One who will help a woman find her identity in Him rather than in men and false securities. He is the only One who can take a woman's desire to travel; and break her heart for nations who do not know the name of Jesus. He is the only One who can convert a woman from dancing on tables in a red dress, to now dancing for joy covered in the scarlet cleansing blood of Jesus Christ. As I write to you these words of encouragement, I also speak them over myself. From the moment we accept Jesus Christ; it no longer matters what we have done or who we once were.

"In Him we have redemption through His blood, the forgiveness of sins, according to the riches of his grace."

Ephesians 1:7 (NKJV)

On the first few mission trips, the Lord has taken me to places, leaving me in awe of His love for us. It was hard to fully comprehend unconditional love until serving children in Latin

America. The Niños have very little, and without hesitation, charge full force wanting to give a stranger a grand amount hugs and adoration. They did not care about the person I was before coming to Christ; or the fact my Spanish was good enough to barely hold a conversation. Each one sat close by inching their way onto my lap searching for a warm embrace from someone who has come a great distance to be with them. A day I will never forget is when the Lord opened an opportunity to use my testimony to help others. Our team went to visit an all-girl's middle school. After playing games and sharing a gospel message, it was time to pray. While holding hands in a circle the Holy Spirit opened my eyes to the hurts of those precious daughters. The pain was undeniably familiar. Without words, we stood arms wrapped; soaking up a wave of comfort over the pain we had laid at our Father's feet. Our lead translator made her way beside me and explained most of the teenage girls were victims of sexual abuse and are often forced into prostitution to financially help their families. In the last minutes; with much needed help from the translator - thank you Jesus, I shared how God forgave me for the years I spent in a red dress living lost and broken. The girls stared wide-eyed with hope as I spoke about how He is the ultimate Redeemer who invites them to also be included into His legacy for a special purpose. Of course, my story does not end there. When God is the author, there are many sequels that will go beyond one woman's chapter. How exciting is that! Not just for Rahab alone; those girls or me; he also includes YOU in His book of life; if you believe Him. Together we can be in confidence, that God can take where we have been, and use it to start a new adventure.

Questions to Reflection

1. Do you feel as though you have taken too many wrong turns in life that God cannot use you?

2. Is there an insecurity in your past and the possibility of it having an effect on where God has placed you?

3. List some of your life experiences. Are there any you see God possibly using to help others?

4. Is there an area in your life that God is asking you to surrender control to him?

5. In what ways have you overcome past wrongdoings through God's Love and forgiveness?

Let us Pray

Father, I humbly come to You. I recognize that You, my Lord, are the One true Author of our lives. Thank you for Your redemption and everlasting love. Forgive me. Please wash clean my history and help rewrite the story of my past to a future that brings You glory. I no longer want to continue trying to write my own version of life. Let this prayer be a declaration of surrendering the pen to You, my God. Amen.

Affirmations

- I am renewed

- I am enlightened

- I release my past

- I am growing in my faith

- I have a God-given purpose

- God is rewriting my story

- Jesus loves me

- I DARE TO BELIEVE!

Helpful Scriptures

- Ephesians 1:7

- Colossians 1:14

- 2 Corinthians 5:17

- Galatians 6:15

- Titus 3:5

- Romans 12:2

My Faith Steps

_____

_____

_____

_____

_____

_____

_____

_____

_____

_____

_____

CHAPTER 5

Author Evelyn P. Andrews

The Walk of Faith

Author Evelyn P. Andrews

Talk about a little girl who just adored her father, that was me. I was a daddy's girl. He was my world. He was kind, funny, patient, and an excellent provider – the ideal father! The laughter from his funny jokes and his overall pleasant demeanor, brought such warmth to our home. It was such a delight to do little things for him like preparing the table with his meals. So, you could imagine my horror, at ten years of age, when I got the dreadful news that my loving thirty-nine-year-old father suddenly died of a heart attack. It felt like my whole world collapsed. My mind was filled with questions. How could this be? Why did this happen? What are we going to do? What is my mommy going to do? I cried, God, we need Your help! It is one of the scariest situations for a child to experience. Fear gripped my little heart. I thought to myself – is this what we need to expect from life? The people we love are just snatched away from us without any warning? It was all confusing to me. I remember thinking of the uncertainty of life.

Dad was the pillar in our family. Everything changed - seemingly overnight. My fate in life changed from being in a family, who were in a financial position to hire several workers to assist in our family business and pay for my education, to now almost scrambling to keep things running and make ends meet. I had to grow up quickly. I eventually ended up dropping out of school to help my mom take care of the home and my younger siblings.

My mom became more special to me after my dad passed. I clung to her more as I got to understand the fragility of life. I started to realize that she had a special gift, where God would give her visions for our family and even of things around the world. Being young, I did not quite understand it all. I clearly remember an older neighbor telling me not to make light of my mom's gifting. He said God has His special people to whom He reveals His secrets and she must be one of those people. I vividly recall some of those events happening, just as she saw it in her vision. It was then that I started to take things of God seriously and began to understand the gifts of the Spirit and how God prepares His people in this walk of faith. I loved my mom dearly and longed to hear what message God was sending through her. That connection time was short-lived because, to my horror, she died of cancer at the age of 45. I was once again, devastated!

As a young woman I was left with a broken heart, losing the very two people that I loved so dearly, and who loved me in return; my mom and dad. Although I had other relatives and a few good friends, I had to face the world without my key support system; but in my heart, I knew I was not alone, the Lord was with me.

Having such a special father gave me high expectations for a life partner. I thought that one day I would find a wonderful husband like my dad and raise a family together, but that was not my story. I trusted some people who were deceitful and filled with ill-intentions, broken promises, and selfishness. Somehow, God turned all of that around for my good.

Although it was met with great displeasure with some folks in my community, I became a single mom to three beautiful daughters that I love very much. They are each unique and special in their own way and I feel blessed to have them in my life.

Being a single mom is no easy feat. There are times you wish there was a partner in the home to help you handle the cares of life. However, once I decided that I was not going to go through any more broken-hearted experiences, I completely committed my life to Christ and have lived a 'sold-out' life to Him. I knew I had to forgive everyone who had hurt me and allow Christ to completely lead my life. There was no turning back for me and I have absolutely no regrets with that decision.

There are so many instances when my faith was tested and I had to stand firm in my belief. This was especially true when our family faced various financial and health crises situations.

One instance was a health crisis with my youngest daughter, Samantha, fondly called Sammy, when she was a baby. Sammy was like a live doll for her sisters. They loved playing with her. My second daughter, Rhonda would go home from school lunchtime just to play with her baby sister. My eldest daughter Bea (Roxy), who is eighteen years older than Sammy was like a second mommy to her. She loved helping to take care of her. She took good care of her for a little while, but she got a part time job and Sammy had to go to a babysitter.

I remember that lunchtime phone call like it was yesterday. It was Rhonda on the other end of the line frantically calling from the babysitter's line, "Mommy, please, please come home quickly! I don't like how Sammy is looking – she is not responding to me – she doesn't even want to play today." The babysitter also agreed that Sammy was not doing well that day.

I immediately asked one or my work contacts to connect me with a good doctor in the city and quickly ran home to get Sammy. When I got there, Rhonda had already dressed her baby sister for the trip to the doctor. As I rushed her to the doctor's office, she was becoming even more droopy and her fever was spiking. Everyone was gasping as I carried this almost lifeless baby into the doctor. My heart sank, as the doctor declared that he was not sure if I would be fortunate to get the required medication in time, for her to live. Then my faith went into overdrive. Something supernatural rose up in me that day. I dared to believe God! I prayed in faith as the tears ran down my face. God, please save my child! My knees became shaky but not my faith. It was as if I did not know how to walk, but I had to take this walk of faith. I grabbed the prescription and stumbled to the pharmacy. It seemed like the longest journey, as I cried out ... God please help me! Please help me to get this medication... and please let it work speedily ... Oh God ... please heal my child!

Everyone was awaiting the death news, but my faith in God was unwavering. I kept declaring Psalm 118:17 over her. Sammy will live and not die and will declare the works of the Lord. The doctor said she would need special care, *if* she happened to survive this advanced viral condition. I wanted to be there with her every step of the way. Roxy, was always extremely bright in both Math and English and was enjoying her first part time job out of high school. Although it didn't pay much, she was excited that it covered her necessary young woman's expenses. She was such a loving and caring sister, that she offered to give up the job to be home with her baby sister. However, as a mother, I felt that I was the one who was obligated to be there with my sick child. No one thought Sammy was going to live, not even the doctor and I was not going to let her out of my sight. This needed 24/7 faith. I was not going give up on her. This was a serious situation and it needed drastic action. I was determined to stand in the gap with prayers and care until she was nursed back to health.

That is when I made the hardest decision a single parent could ever make. I quit my job without knowing how I was going to pay all the bills and take care of my family. At that moment, all I knew was I had to be there for my sick child. This was going to be a complete walk of faith. Through much prayer and standing in faith, to everyone's surprise, Sammy slowly came back to health. God proved Himself as Jehovah Rapha; her healer. My faith in God grew even stronger as I saw Him perform that miracle, I knew He was going to provide for my family. I knew He was getting ready to take me on another journey to prove that He was, not only faithful as Jehovah Rapha, but He was going to be faithful as Jehovah Jireh; our Provider. Every gift that He placed in me came alive, as I found ways to work from home, sewing, making crafts and snacks for sale.

Every day He provided for us in miraculous ways. Some days were harder than others. Many times, my back was against the wall with the emotional and financial hardship, but I continued to walk by faith every day and God came through every time. The scripture 2 Corinthians 5:7 became my reality:

"For we walk by faith, not by sight NKJV."

*****

Once my children were grown, most of our struggles were over. God turned around everything the enemy meant for evil in my life and made it good. As I look at Sammy now, I understand why the enemy tried to cut her purpose short. She is now fulfilling her God-given purpose in caring for those who are sick. She has been a registered nurse for the past 20 years, serving most of those years in the United Kingdom. She has a compelling passion for saving lives, and is truly the hands of Jesus, to so many who desperately need it.

As I reflect on my life, I remember excessively thinking of the uncertainty of life, as a child and young woman when my parents died. After having children, there were times when I wondered if that was going to be my fate too? I could not let those fears hang over me. I had to be bold in this faith walk. My parents' fate did not have to be mine. I was in the hands of God and I was determined to be who I was destined to be, and I threw aside those worries. God was gracious to preserve my life to see this ripe old age of eighty-four years, in relatively perfect health. Every day I give him thanks for His goodness.

Although my journey was not filled with all glorious experiences, my good days have far exceeded my difficult ones. I saw the hand of God throughout my life and I am grateful. My latter days are truly greater than my past. One of the best decisions I ever made in life was accepting the Lord Jesus as my Savior. It helped me to brave the storms of life and guide my family in the ways of the Lord.

I am so thankful for the church family who helped my family with the spiritual aspect of their lives. I could not do it alone and they have played a pivotal role in my children's faith in the Lord. They went to Sunday School, youth service, and every church event and all were baptized and accepted Jesus as Lord and Savior. I even remember the pastor, Bishop John Cummings coming to our home to pray for Sammy when she was a toddler and she complained of seeing creatures and having nightmares. His declaration after praying was one of faith "Samantha, from today nothing will scare you anymore" and just as he said it, so it was!

I realized my ministry was never going to be one in the forefront and I am quite content with that calling. My passion is prayer; for leaders, to see their ministries blossom, and for people to see God bring them hope, healing and deliverance. It is not even important for them to hear me praying for them. My obligation is to my God and that He hears me when I call. There is power in that secret place of prayer! In your personal "war room". There are so many prayers that God has answered and I continue to expect breakthroughs for more, by His grace and for His glory. When I see the results, I often look up and smile and just say, thank you Jesus for showing yourself as real again!

God would often lead me to strangers, some at their wits end with life. I would arrive just in time to build their faith in God – to help save their lives and bring them hope. I have shared some of those stories in detail in another 2021 book release called, *"Empowered to Overcome Tough Seasons of Life"* compiled by Rhonda P. Fraser.

Like my mom, God began to visit me too with dreams and visions of things to come. One instance, where I experienced that firsthand, was the day my daughter Rhonda was born. The day of her birth, I saw a vision of a "Man" (must be the angel of the Lord); all dressed in white as His garment swirled my way as He placed this most beautiful baby girl in my lap. Not long after, I was holding the exact baby in real life. I tell her very often, ever since she was very young, it does not matter what you aspire to do in life, you came here to do a special work for the Lord. Believe it and walk in it! You are one of God's gifts to this world! I believe that vision and those words of encouragement to my daughter has led her to embrace the calling of God on her life. She explained how my encounter with the angel of the Lord pushes her through rejection and other tough seasons to do what He has called her to do. She explains some of it in the bestseller books that she co-authored *"This Is How I Fight My Battles,"* compiled by Kenise Etwaru and *"Women of War: Peace in the Midst of the Storm."* compiled by Dr. Delene Musielak.

Today I am glad I held onto my faith. I am thankful that I fought for my children, even when at times it seemed most sacrificial. My eldest has the most amazing sense of humor and infectious laughter. She could brighten your day with those warm conversations and jokes that every elderly mother enjoys. Together with her siblings, they compete in spoiling me. Whenever they try to probe to see what I need, my response is always, I need nothing. I am happy and content with my life and where God has brought me. The love and support over the years from friends, loved ones, especially my children, grandchildren, extended family, in-laws, especially my son-in-law, Rev. Reginald Fraser is priceless! My earnest desire is to see people serving Jesus. That would be the greatest gift I could ever receive from all of you. If that is the only takeaway you receive from this chapter. Then my contribution here is complete!

To every single mother or anyone out there, facing the pangs of life, those who question your purpose and wonder if you could make this walk of faith, I say yes, you can! I am a witness that it is worth it and God will help you. Just Believe and keep pressing on in faith! This is not the time for giving up.

One day you when you are older, you will be glad that you held onto His promises. There is glory on the other side of pain. Psalms 30:5 reminds us that "weeping may endure for the night, but joy comes in the morning NKJV." Be encouraged and continue boldly in your Walk of Faith! Your joy is coming and it may be sooner than you think! JUST BELIEVE!

Questions for Reflection

1. Do you have to handle your responsibilities without a reliable partner to help you?

2. Do you feel the pain from losing a loved one and cannot seem to figure out how to move forward?

3. Is there a time when you had to make a sacrificial decision for your loved one? Perhaps, giving up a job, possession, or some opportunity? Maybe your health has suffered as a result of some stress you endured.

4. Do you have a loved one who was given a detrimental health prognosis?

5. Do you believe that the Lord can help you in all these situations?

Let us Pray

Dear Lord, I bring everyone in need of prayer for some situation that I mentioned. I ask that you prove yourself as the God who could reach them at the point of their need. As they dare to take this walk of faith, prove to them that it is not in vain. Reveal your miracle-working nature so they could trust you even more. I pray you provide for their needs. For those who are hurting, sick or have lost loved ones, bring healing, comfort and assurance. To those who are in bondage, bring deliverance. To those who feel like life was unfair, those who had to make great sacrifices for others, restore the "lost" time and give them a good harvest. To those who feel alone, prove Yourself as "Emanuel", the God Who is always with us. Give them a testimony today, in the Name of Jesus. Amen.

Affirmations

- I am walking in faith

- I am not alone; God is with me

- I am creative

- I am enough

- I am determined

- I inspire others

- I will live out my purpose

- I am healthy

- I let go of hurts

- I am fulfilled in Christ

- I DARE TO BELIEVE

Helpful Scriptures

- 2 Corinthians 5:7

- Isaiah 40:31

- Job 8:7

- Philippians 3:13-14

- Psalm 55:22

- Philippians 4:19

My Faith Steps

_____

_____

_____

_____

_____

_____

_____

_____

_____

_____

CHAPTER 6

Author Heather Barfield

You Are a Daughter of Destiny

Author Heather Barfield

I am a Daughter of Destiny. My story does not begin with my birth, but with my mother's birth. My mother was born out of wedlock. This might not seem like such of a scandalous thing in this current age, but I assure you that in 1924 and with West Indian/Caribbean heritage, this was indeed a big thing.

I was born in the beautiful country of Barbados, the third of three children. My maternal grandmother was born there too. When my grandmother was a young woman, she decided that Barbados was too small for her. Against her Christian parents' wishes, she ventured out of Barbados and traveled to the United States of America. She would never return. She arrived at Ellis Island when she was just 19 years old. As she explored life and was learning to take care of herself far from the supervision of her Christian parents, she met a man and became pregnant with my mother. She never married this man and my mother subsequently never knew her father, never even knew his name. My mother was born in the United States so by reason of birth she automatically became an American citizen. My grandmother, still struggling to survive herself, did not want the responsibility of a child and the decision was made to send my mother as a baby to Barbados to be raised by her grandparents. Her grandparents; my great-grandparents, loved the Lord and raised my mother as their own. My mother was raised in a loving Christian family. My mother always referred to her grandparents as her parents and lovingly called them Mame and Pa.

It was very significant that my mother was an American citizen. Many years later, after she married my dad and gave birth to her three children, the decision was made that they would leave Barbados for a better education for their children and a better life in the "States". At that time, leaving Barbados to travel to other countries for what was perceived as 'a better life' was very popular. Many Bajans chose to travel to either England or the United States of America; but with either choice, there was difficulty because one still had to have a visa or be sponsored by a person of that country. However, because my mother was born in the United States and already had U.S. citizenship, the path was clear for her to come to America. She did not need to be sponsored by anyone.

When my mother arrived in the United States, she stayed with friends; found employment, and a year later sponsored her husband and three children to join her in America. I was only four years old when we arrived in the United States. My father purchased a brownstone house in Brooklyn, New York for us to live. After that, one of the first things my father did was seek out a church for the family to attend for worship. As Anglicans we joined an Episcopal church in walking distance to our home. Every Saturday night my siblings and I prepared to go to church the next morning. This was just a part of our lives. Like clockwork; Sunday mornings we were off to church. We did not just attend the service; we also attended Sunday School before the Sunday service.

In Sunday School I learned about the characters in the Bible and about God's love. Many concepts were not new to me because I had heard these stories in my home. I also heard my mom and dad praying to their Jesus. My mother told me stories of how her grandparents would talk to Jesus first thing in the morning and even throughout the day. Prayer was an active part of their lives. This created in me a curiosity—I found myself asking "how do you talk to Jesus?"

I believe my grandmother's travel to the United States; my mother's birth there, and her being raised by her grandparents were all orchestrated by God. It was part of His divine plan to get me into position - to get me where He wanted me to be - to get me to America to live a life of ministry.

If my grandmother had not rebelled; if she had not decided to leave her home in Barbados and travel to the United States, I would not be here. If she had not made the decision to send her daughter, my mother, back to Barbados to live with her godly grandparents, I would not be here. If my great-grandparents had not accepted my mom as a child born out of wedlock; I would not be here. If my parents had not decided to make the sacrifice to leave Barbados to come to America for a better life; I would not be here ministering today.

What am I saying? – I am a Daughter of Destiny. My mother was a Daughter of Destiny. God orchestrated her birth in the United States. He orchestrated the open door that she would later use to bring her family to America. There was a plan and a purpose for my life before I was ever born; before my mother was even born. If you are here; no matter the circumstance of your birth, you are a Daughter of Destiny. God did not make a mistake when you were born. Even if you were born out of wedlock; were rejected by your own mother as a baby; if you never knew your father; were adopted; you are not an accident or a mistake.

You are a Daughter of Destiny. Perhaps you have suffered some family drama or trauma and you are asking God *"why?"* Perhaps you were a child of divorced parents; you fell into alcoholism or struggled with drugs, no matter your individual circumstance, regardless of your mistakes and missteps; God still loves you. God redeems and God restores. He still has a plan for your life.

My mother struggled with rejection from her mother; but God gave her the grace to forgive. God brought her through those times and into a better life. He gave her faith and allowed her to see a vision for her life; a life that is happy, loved and prosperous. She led a long and full life, going to her eternal reward at the age of 90; and leaving a legacy of prayer and trust in God. Her marriage of 58 years to my dad produced three successful children and five successful grandchildren. I will be eternally grateful to my mother for finding the strength and courage to make the heart wrenching decision to be separated from her three small children and her husband, for a whole year and travel to America. She did not know what life would bring, but trusted God to go before her, to lead, guide and direct her. I am a naturalized citizen of the United States of America and proud of it.

As a Daughter of Destiny, I believe God was calling me to Himself before I ever accepted Him as my Lord and Savior. As a young teenager I was sure that I knew everything; when in fact, I knew nothing at all. I pretended I had it all together; but inwardly,

I was miserable. I had many questions and no answers. Is this all there is to life? I had no purpose or direction. I felt lonely; even with people all around me. I felt that no one understood me. I was on a lonely road going nowhere, unhappy and bored with life. My feeling of loneliness and lack of self-worth was the enemy's deception. I fell for it; until one day it all changed.

Living with Christian parents meant I was exposed to many opportunities to hear the Gospel of Jesus Christ. My parents; in particular, loved the evangelist Billy Graham and would often watch his televised church services. I often sat with my parents as they watched those church services. One day, as I was watching one of the church services, I heard an invitation to come follow Jesus. It was not the first time I heard this invitation, but *this* time it was different. I felt desperate and was sick and tired of being sick and tired. As Billy Graham gave the altar call to accept Jesus, the song "Just as I Am" tugged at my spirit, but I resisted the call. The tugging became so persistent that after the program ended, I could not get the invitation to follow Jesus out of my mind.

Not responding to the tug made me even more miserable. So, I finally gave in. I went into my bedroom; alone in the dark and quiet of that room, I knelt down by the side of my bed and prayed a very simple prayer: "Jesus if you are real, come into my life.

Forgive me. I want to receive You." In that moment I started to weep; not tears of sadness, but of pure joy. It was like a weight that I had been carrying suddenly fell off of me. I felt a joy and a peace that I had not known before. I was made a new creature that day and began to walk as a Daughter of Destiny. I have followed hard after Jesus ever since.

We do not often see God's plan at a glance. We especially do not see it at the beginning; when we are first learning to trust Him, but God is the Alpha and the Omega; the Beginning and the End. He knows the end from the beginning, and He plans accordingly. God's plan for your life is good. God is the ultimate planner and He has a great plan for your life; from the cradle to the grave. As you trust God with your life, you will experience His best plan. God says in Jeremiah 29:11 "For I know the thoughts I think toward you, says the Lord, thoughts of peace and not of evil, to give you a future and a hope (NKJV)." His best plan always comes to pass no matter how many twists, turns, delays, or redirections we may take through disobedience or plots of the enemy. In Romans 8:28, "...all things work together for good to those who love God, to those who are called according to His purpose (NKJV)." This scripture is so important to remember, along with Jeremiah. 29:11 because God works life out for your good. God is good; not part of the time; not even some of the time, but *all* of the time. So, keep this in mind as you go through life's bumpy, sometimes rollercoaster roads. Hang on for the ride, never stop trusting God, never stop believing His plan is to prosper you, to give you a hope and a future.

Over the years, I have given God the little that I have and He has made it grand. Today, I am a pastor and have a women's empowerment ministry called Daughters of Destiny. As a conference host and speaker, God has used me to impart life and bring encouragement into the lives of many women. I am also a published author; a retired public-school teacher, and a mother of two adult sons. So, do not give up. Be encouraged. Give God praise for the little that you have; allow Him to use it for His glory. God is not a respecter of persons. What He does for one; He will do for another.

Are you a Daughter of Destiny? God wants you to know that He loves you. He not only loves you; but has a good and perfect plan and purpose for your life. It may not be as straight of a line as you think. It might have zig-zag lines; have snags and loose threads running through it. It might even have unforeseen threads of different shapes, colors and sizes. However, when you turn the tapestry of your life around and you see the other side; from God's perspective, then you will see the beauty that He has made. God will reveal to you the masterpiece He is making of your life. You will see that you are a Daughter of Destiny.

Questions for Reflection

1. Are you a Daughter of Destiny?

2. How do you know?

3. Take a moment to ask God right now:

   - What is my destiny?

   - What would you have me to do?

4. God says in Jeremiah 29:11: "I know the plans I have for you."

   - Do you know what plan God has for you?

   - Write down what God is saying to you about His plans for your life.

5. Who do you have to forgive for rejecting, hurting, disappointing, or betraying you?

   - Ask God to help you to forgive them; take that step and forgive them.

   - Matthew 6:14-15 admonishes us to forgive others even as God forgives us.

Let us Pray

Dear Lord Jesus, I surrender my 'little' to you. I trust You to make it grand. Thank you for the perfect plan you have for my life. I ask You to forgive me; even as I forgive others who have hurt me. I ask You to come into my heart and make me a new creature. I want to live for You from this day forward. I want to be a Daughter of Destiny. Amen.

Affirmations

- I am positioned by God

- I am forgiving

- I am resilient

- I am a Daughter of Destiny

- I am a child of God

- I am a child of destiny

- I DARE TO BELIEVE!

Helpful Scriptures

- Proverbs 3:5-6

- Psalm 138:8

- Ephesians 2:10

- Matthew 6:14-15

- Job 42:2

My Faith Steps

CHAPTER 7

Author Marsha Winters

Every Victory Comes from a Battle

Author Marsha Winters

Do we admire someone's victory without knowing their battles? In I Samuel in the Bible, we read how the prophet Samuel's life proved important, as he was the only one to anoint the first and second king of Israel. We read his story, but can easily miss the trials that Hannah; his mother, went through to birth her destiny.

Being in quarantine during 2020, gave me the opportunity to spend much more time with my four children. Hikes, laser tag, movies, card games, board games, and a lot of baking, allowed me to make pleasant memories with them. Before quarantine, I worked at our church's private school, while pursuing my degree, and managed our fairly new ministry called, *Through the Winters.*

Being married to my favorite pastor and my best friend for over 20 years has been a ministry in and of itself, as we venture daily in efforts to help others pursue a better version of themselves. Despite all that was on my plate, I tried to make sure that I was there for our four children by paying attention to their needs, cares, tears, and fears. I missed it many times but I am glad that what I missed; God caught.

My oldest daughter stuck closest with me during this time as we worked together on her culinary assignments for school, which she needed to fulfill before graduation. With her dating her first boyfriend, she had many questions that led to serious conversations on the topic of marriage, parenting, and how her father and I handled life's challenges. One day she asked my advice on some things which started one of those 'heart-to-heart' talks. I told her that what her father and I had, was not something that you get overnight. It took work and obedience. Hours after our amazing talk, I was surprised to walk into the kitchen to see her eyes red and her face moist from tears. "Are you okay?", I asked. She hesitantly shook her head, "No." I asked myself, "What could have happened? Did she fight with her boyfriend? Was it one of her friends?" I asked, "What happened?" She waited a little and then, with tears filling her eyes again, she answered, "I don't think I could ever be as good as you. You always have time for us. You always know the right things to say. I don't know if I could ever be like you." I was not expecting her to say that. I never try to present myself as 'perfect' or as 'having everything all together', but in her eyes, she saw something different. She was viewing my victories, without understanding my battles.

Going back in time when I was 16 years old, I remember being away at the annual youth convention held in Syracuse, New York; by the New York Network of the Assembly of God. On the second night; after the preaching, I responded to the altar call, just as about a hundred other teens did. At that time, I had little hope in my heart that God could help me. I walked in faith to the altar, but I was dealing with doubt, fear, and emotional baggage. My identity was lost and nothing in me knew what God could do with someone like me. However, I was going to take Him up on His promise. What promise you ask? Well, let me tell you of the day I almost gave up.

A year and a half before this trip, I was home in my bathroom with the door closed. I examined blood that had leaked in my mouth from my busted lip. My face was swollen on the left side. There were occasions where he had beat me so bad that I could not hold my bowels; he found this hilarious. He drank, did drugs, and got himself involved with the wrong crowd; which put our family in danger for a season. On this particular day, my father had beaten me up like I was a stranger from the street. He threw me on my bed, got on top of me, slapped my face, and punched me straight in the mouth causing my teeth to split my upper and lower lip.

I had to figure out a way to survive the blows by promising myself that I would never cry again during the moments he was abusing me. If he was not breaking me down with his fists, belts, or anything else he found; he used his words. After this particular beating, my father decided his fist were not enough. He proceeded to curse at me and degraded everything about me. He made it clear that I was "good-for-nothing". In the middle of him calling me whatever he felt like, the phone rang. It was for me. I was horrified as he continued to ruin my self-image by repeating all those obscenities to…who knows who it was on the other end. He ranted and raved about what he planned to do to me because I was so worthless. When he was done, he hung up on the person. It was no secret. Everyone knew I was abused. Teachers saw it from gashes on my neck that I tried to cover up with turtlenecks. Cruel peers would laugh at me when they saw my bruises, welts, and slashes on my arms and legs. I could never get away from the truth. I was "one of *those* kids". So, to know that a friend or even someone I cared about, had called me and experienced my father's rage and hatred for me, was more humiliating than I could ever explain. I was going to have to go to school or church and wonder who it was that figured it out. Could we not fight in secret?

Has your battle caused you embarrassment? Hannah faced her own embarrassment, when it was clear to her and her husband, that she was barren. She lived with such humiliation as her husband pursued a second wife to carry on his legacy. Where did Hannah's embarrassment lead her?

My humiliation led me to a point where I genuinely prayed a prayer I had never prayed before. That night I got up and turned on the light next to my bed very quietly. My brothers were fast asleep as I wrote a letter to each person in my family, letting them know how much they meant to me. Tears streamed down my eyes as I thought of being free from this world. I could not believe the sense of joy that flooded my thoughts as I imagined the next time, I was going to open my eyes it would be in Heaven.

So how was I planning to leave this world? I was going to plead my case to God that I had no reason for being here. After writing the letter I cried ever so silently as I prayed like I had never prayed before, "God take my life!" My pain brought me to plead for death, but Hannah's pain brought her to the Temple. Our locations were different, but we were both desperate for God to help remove our pain. Hannah prayed violently - yet ever so silently - so violently that she was accused of being drunk. How did Hannah overcome this battle?

After pleading my case to God of how my life was meaningless, worthless, and heading down a path that was going to lead to death, I went back to sleep with great expectation of waking up in Heaven. "How would I die?" I was somehow convinced that God would not dismiss my request.

Since you're reading this, you know the ultimate outcome. That next morning, I woke with the sun shining in on my face and heard movement in my house. My older brother got ready for his daily routine and my mom was getting ready for work. I had never felt so betrayed. How could God do this to me? There was no reason for living anymore. I sat in my bed as tears ran down my face. "How could You do this to me? Don't you get it?! I don't want to be here anymore!" My anger was ablaze as I sat there wondering how I was going to get through a day I did not plan to face. Hannah was faced with a priest that accused her of being drunk, but God used him to speak to her. Like Hannah, I too, heard God speak very gently to me, "There will be a death in your family, but it won't be you. I have a plan for you; a family for you. Your time here is not over." How was I going to process God placing His will over mine? Have you ever had to submit your will to God to overcome the battles you have faced? I would love to say that His words left me hopeful and ready for what life had for me, but it did not. Inside I was dying no matter what I showed people on the outside. I did not believe anything He said about having a plan for me until that day at the On-Center in Syracuse. Death did hit my home, just as God said. My father died seven months after I asked God to take my life and at the age of 16; a year and a half later, I desperately wanted to hear what plans He had for me. He saved me but saved me for what?

I remember crying as I responded to the altar call. I made my way down to the arena floor; wondering what He had for me. I first needed to weep through my doubt and ask for forgiveness for not believing Him. As I knelt on that cold floor, the Lord told me He was going to use me in ministry; as He took my story to set others free. I continued to be overwhelmed as He gave me a quick glimpse of my future; the family he had for me. For a quick minute, I felt a joy and peace that was mine; perhaps similar to how Hannah felt when the priest Eli told her that God had heard her prayer. Hannah had no evidence she was going to get that child she wanted but peace and comfort overtook her unbelief and doubt.

As I wept and finally accepted that He had something for me, a hand touched my shoulder and lifted me up from the floor. It was my spiritual father; my youth pastor. At that moment he gave me a hug while I cried with joy at the life God had for me. God sent him over to be His hands and arms for me.

I began to wonder, how was I going to overcome such a huge battle of severe abuse? Twenty-two years later, my eyes welled up when my oldest daughter thought she could never be as good as me. If only she could have seen where I was mentally, emotionally and spiritually at her age. What I have with her was birthed out of obedience to God. I wanted to be everything that my father said I was not. Hannah was provoked and I made my mistakes, lost my temper, thought the wrong thoughts but I did not need to have an example of good parenting to be a good parent. I wish my kids could understand that they are miracles I can hold. What God did for me He can do for others as well. I dare you to believe!

I may not know your story—nor the struggles you face—but I do know that God is real; He proved it to me and he could do the same for you. He has a great plan for your life and is ready and willing to help you. Would you embrace it today? Do not believe the lies of the enemy that you are worthless. You are worthy; beautiful and precious. Do not allow the enemy to shortcut your purpose because of those painful experiences. God creates powerful testimonies out of the ugliness of broken lives. He offers victory to fighters who obey Him. Don't give up! There is Hope in God! Dare to Believe Him!

Questions for Reflection

1. Do you find yourself comparing your life to others, not knowing the storms that they have passed through?

2. Have you ever been ashamed of a battle that you faced?

3. Do you think everyone sees and knows your battle, so shame has overcome you?

4. Is your pain so great that you cannot see further than today? God can help you. Note: There is also additional professional help that could help you through this process. You do not have to feel stigmatized.

5. Has the enemy whispered lies about your worth and purpose?

6. Do not let your trials and tribulation push you to give up. Hannah was pushed to the temple. Where does your battle lead you?

7. If God were to give you a glimpse of His promise, what would that look like? Are you willing to see that promise come through?

Let us Pray

God you are amazing! Just as You have been faithful to me in my darkest times, You can do the same thing for my friends who are desperately in need of your divine intervention. I do not know if they are looking at others' successes and thinking that they can never reach victory; but God, You know that You have a plan for them. I pray for hope if they are feeling hopeless. I pray for victory where they may feel defeated. I speak life where they feel there is only death and I rebuke the work of darkness. Wrap Your arms around them and let them know that You understand every tear and every groan. Assure them that they do not have to walk this road alone; as You will walk it with them. Send support and give them guidance through their valley season. I know that You are going to do great things if they are willing to obey and believe You. Thank you for everything You have done and what You are going to do in Jesus' Name, Amen.

Affirmations

- I am worthy

- I am loved

- I am blessed with life

- I have a great future

- I am hopeful

- I am beautiful

- I am delivered

- I speak God's plan over my life

- I believe God's plan for my life

- I embrace wholesome thoughts and rebuke wrong thoughts

- I bring value to this world

- I have a unique purpose

- I am grateful to be alive

- Jesus loves me

- I DARE TO BELIEVE!

Helpful Scriptures

- Romans 8:31

- Philippians 4:13

- Revelations 21:4

- Psalm 34:18

- Psalm 147:3

- Isaiah 33:2

- Romans 5:5

- Philippians 4:13

My Faith Steps

_____

_____

_____

_____

_____

_____

_____

_____

_____

_____

_____

CHAPTER 8

Author Heather Meyerend

Thriving through Setbacks

Author Heather Meyerend

I have always loved words. I enjoyed reading and could often be found totally immersed in a library book; sometimes to the neglect of my childhood chores. I was inspired by my high school English teacher and planned on a life in academia; likely teaching English, but God has a way of taking us down paths we least expect.

I had a great plan for my life; or so I thought, when I migrated to the United States of America from the beautiful island of Jamaica. In the beginning, I was enjoying the freedom of the extra time spent with the Lord in my daily devotions, while looking for temporary work. I was offered a job at a nursing home as an Aide, but declined based on the feedback from my older sister about its difficulty and non-suitability for me. I took the next offered position as a clerical worker in at a large insurance company, but a seed in the medical care field was planted in my spirit that I could not shake, which would later blossom into a career in nursing.

I remember praying one morning and specifically asking God for direction as to what career to pursue, and the verse that I was led to I Thessalonians 2:7, "But we were gentle among you just as a nursing mother cherishes her own children (NKJV)," was a clear call to pursue nursing. I was overjoyed that the Lord would speak so clearly to me and in such a way that I had no doubt that it was Him. A career in nursing was the farthest occupation from my mind, but I embraced it because I trusted that my heavenly Father knew best. I began applying to colleges and then tragedy struck our family and all plans were put on hold.

My beloved older brother, Noel, died tragically at the age of 24 while out swimming with friends. I vividly remember the knock on the door and my mother falling to her knees with deep, groans as two sad-eyed young men gave us the tragic news. This came as an immense shock followed by disbelief. My mother and I held each other and cried. "They must be mistaken. How could this be happening again?" We had already experienced multiple losses in our family and the pain was distressingly familiar, and no less shocking.

How do you process the death of a brother in the prime of his life? Was my faith resilient enough to withstand these tragedies? Would I sink down in despair; questioning God or would my faith take me yet again through another 'valley of the shadow of death?' When I had no more words or tears and had no answers to the "why" questions, I had learned to live with the lingering questions and was determined to trust God through this storm. I believed that the One who had been faithful to me before was the same God who would carry me through, again. These lines from the song. "He's Been Faithful" became so real: *"He's Been Faithful to Me. Looking back, His love and mercy I see. Though in my heart I have questioned, even failed to believe. Yet He's been faithful to me."*

All of our plans of pooling resources to buy a home and move from our cramped living quarters received a severe setback. In time, we regrouped as a family. With my mother's encouragement, I pursued my God-given dream and became a registered nurse. During this period of living under very humble circumstances and enduring the immigrant experience, I felt sustained by God despite winters without heat; and sometimes without hot water, a leaking roof and dealing with a landlord who seemed to have no pity. In Jamaica we lacked nothing, but in New York, it seemed as if privation was everywhere. During these difficult years we learned to laugh at the ridiculousness of our situation as we opened the umbrella to get from one room to the next when it rained heavily. At some point, it seemed as if we were living in an abandoned building. "Where was the Landlord?" we asked; but that setback was only for a season.

During those difficult years in New York, I was encouraged by God's promise to the Israelites, who were also "immigrants" to a foreign land, where He said in Jeremiah 29:11 "For I know the thoughts I think toward you, says the Lord, thoughts of peace and not of evil, to give you a future and a hope (NKJV)." Hardships, disappointments, tragedies, twists and turns in life have a way of refining us; stripping away pretenses and leaving us wholly vulnerable and dependent on God. Rather than pining for a lost life; a previously comfortable life, the child of God who recognizes that seasons are time-limited and serve a particular good purpose, will thrive through adversity. The exiled immigrants in Babylon who looked ahead to the future and the hope, that God had for them, went on to plant gardens; build houses; marry, and ultimately make a difference in their city.

My beautiful God-given career as a nurse served me well as I moved to California to prepare for missions, or so I thought. I again felt the uprooting and being transplanted into a different culture and the strange feeling of trying to fit in. I immersed myself in studies at Fuller Theological Seminary; made friends in the culture and attempted to thrive. This was a time of testing and stretching as I navigated full time work while carrying a full load of courses at Fuller. This season tested my psychological and emotional well-being and I felt the need to process all of this with a Christian counselor.

My faith grew stronger as I recognized the reality of spiritual warfare. I realized how critical it was to be firmly established in the word of God and in community with other believers. A newfound sense of joy and purpose began to grow within as I recognized God had brought me through an emotionally stormy and disruptive season. Storms are often unexpected and ferocious. We wonder if we will survive; but because we have a loving Heavenly Father who has a greater purpose for us, we can say, "this is only for a season." Storms eventually blow over. The damage is repaired, and lives continue on course just the way God planned. When the Apostle Paul boarded a ship to take him to Rome, he had no doubt that he would arrive at his destination. God had a purpose for him that could not be thwarted by the enemy's destructive threats. No voyage is without its share of difficulties; however, there is an assurance in the purposes of God that anchors our hope during those difficult passages.

It was in this new season that God did something both delightful and unexpected. He introduced me to my future husband. Someone who shared my dream of going on missions overseas. How awesome is our God who could bring two people from totally different cultures yet who had so much in common? A white man from Philadelphia, preparing for missions in the Middle

East, intersecting with a black woman from the Caribbean hoping to fulfill the call of God to the same group of people. God's purposes are not always clear at the outset. We make our plans, but God has the final say. Proverbs 16:1 tells us that, "The preparation of the heart belongs to man, but the answer of the tongue is from the Lord (NKJV)." This was certainly true for us.

While making the rounds to various churches to gain monthly support, it became increasingly clear that we were not meeting our goals, in addition to other obstacles along the way. In the midst of this God wonderfully blessed us with our first-born son, David. The visa we applied for never materialized and a clear word came from the Lord through my pastor in Brooklyn that God had given him our visa and that we should move to Brooklyn and God would make everything clear to us. Needless to say, we were sorely disappointed, but in obedience we packed up and moved to Brooklyn not knowing what God would do.

This was a puzzling new season. Where would this take us? Brooklyn? This was not my plan nor my husband's. What was God up to? With no job; no place to live, and a one-year-old and another baby on the way; we reluctantly moved to Brooklyn. God provided a place for us to live and jobs in quick succession. For about a year, the only message we heard was "when everything seems to be going wrong, it's alright because God is in control." Over time my husband was appointed Principal of Christian Heritage Academy by our Bishop, a position he held for many years until the school closed. He is now impacting the lives of young people in a local Catholic School where he has the liberty to share the love of Christ with them. Our Bishop often jokes "God needed a principal for the Academy, so he sent me to California to bring him to Brooklyn." We are now part of the leadership team at Christian Heritage Ministries, serving in multiple capacities as Teacher, Mission and Prayer Team Leader.

Ministry requires a great deal of patience, compassion, and the ability to empathize; often a gentle presence that speaks calm and comfort. Our world today is very divisive with strident voices vying for our allegiance, but Christ calls us to set a different tone. My sometimes, bewildering experiences bring a certain flavor to my conversations and actions. As a leader, I recognize that setbacks are part and parcel of the human experience and I can therefore bring authenticity and transparency to the conversation. This is the point when breakthrough is likely to occur.

I have also had the privilege of making several mission trips to Ghana, Nigeria, Mexico, Jamaica and Haiti to share the love of Jesus Christ to the broken, lost, and disenfranchised people. I have found the experience deeply rewarding. I see how God uses our experiences to ultimately bring the Kingdom of God close to people so that they too will experience God's redemptive grace. Having dealt with so many losses in my life, it is not surprising, in retrospect, that I was drawn to the work of Hospice; taking care of the dying and providing comfort to those anticipating the death of a loved one.

In my work as a Hospice nurse, I have been able to quickly find common ground with those facing death and the families who are experiencing the unknown territory of life without their loved one. There is a strange satisfaction of knowing that I have been able to journey with someone down this inevitable path, and at times, be the one there holding that person's hand and praying as they took that final breath. My work and call as a Hospice nurse were recognized and written about in The New Yorker magazine - *The Threshold. A Hospice Nurse Encounters*. I believe that the compassion that God has given me, because of my experiences has helped me to make a profound difference in the lives of my patients.

We may never know why God changed our course and redirected us to Brooklyn, but I do know that joy and contentment are found when you are in the center of God's will; whether that is

North Africa or Brooklyn, New York where we have the potential to reach people and groups from all over the world.

Looking back over these experiences, I sometimes wonder what would have been the trajectory of my life, had I returned to Jamaica, as my father suggested. My story would be significantly different in ways, I can only imagine. Yet God, in His infinite grace never shows us the full picture and this becomes our protection. Resilient Faith helps us to thrive even in setbacks. Our difficult experiences become a launching pad for God to accomplish His greater purpose in and through us; purpose that will surely impact untold lives for generations to come. Dare to believe it!

Questions for Reflection

1. Think of a time when you were certain that God was leading you in a particular direction and then discovered this was not God's plan for you. How can you learn to distinguish between your plans and God's plans?

2. When you face setbacks – storms of life – loss, lack, re-direction, what can you do to keep from despair?

3. How can you encourage yourself or help someone who is grieving and unable to move on?

4. Rather than asking why is this happening to me, how can you look for God's purposes in your experience?

5. We all go through tough times. How can you reach out to someone else who might be experiencing severe storms in their life?

Let us Pray

Dear Lord, so many of my experiences seem to be so difficult and I wonder the purpose behind them. Lord, what I do know and affirm is what the scriptures tell me, that though I walk through the darkest valleys I will not be afraid and that You are with me. May I rest in this precious promise. I believe you will help me through the storms that I am now experiencing and will bring me to a safe haven. I know that I will not be in stuck in setbacks, but you will bring great purpose out of it. I ask that you provide me with the right job that aligns with your plan for me. I ask that you direct me to my life partner. I pray you comfort and strengthen me during the grief of losing a loved one. I pray that I will thrive through all my setbacks. May Your greater purpose be accomplished in my life and those around me.

Amen.

Affirmations

- I am thriving

- God's hand is upon my life

- I receive God's comfort

- I am progressing

- My setbacks are stepping stones

- I am seeing God's favor

- I am fulfilling my purpose

- God's divine plan is evolving

- I DARE TO BELIEVE!

Helpful Scriptures

- Prov 16:1-3

- Isaiah 50:7

- James 1:5

- Acts 27:25

- Hebrews 11:6

- 2 Corinthians 4:8,9

- Isaiah 61:3

- Matthew 5:4

- Jeremiah 29:11-13

- Prov 3:5-7

- Luke 4:18

- Hebrews 13:16

- Colossians 1:10

My Faith Steps

_____

_____

_____

_____

_____

_____

_____

_____

_____

_____

CHAPTER 9

Author Eileen Howarth

WIN-WIN Situation: Miraculous Faith

Author Eileen Howarth

Have you ever received bad news? A bad report? Have you ever struggled through a battle? I want to encourage you as a believer to put your faith and trust in the Lord Jesus Christ alone, no matter what bad report; tumultuous situation; terminal infirmity, or life circumstance that causes you to struggle to just get by.

I had been saved and serving the Lord for about ten years when I found myself having severe headaches. I went to the doctor and was diagnosed with a malignant brain tumor. The location of the tumor made it impossible for my doctor to operate, so he prescribed a regimen of chemotherapy and radiation. These treatments lasted about one and a half years. I found myself losing weight, having hair loss, and having no appetite. Through this trial, I called upon the Lord. I studied His Word, and I believed His promises! Now, it was time to trust His Word!

I truly believed He is Jehovah Rapha, my Healer. I kept hearing what the Lord had spoken to my heart about all that He had for me to do for Him, to serve and glorify Him. There were many times that the Lord used someone to speak words over me and declare that the Lord had much work for me to do in His Kingdom. This was just confirming what He had already spoken to my heart. So now as I faced this trial, how could I possibly carry out the work that He had called me to do? I recalled and spoke those words over and over, and I would pray, "Lord if You have spoken these words for my life, then Your plan and purpose is for me to continue serving You. This cannot be the end of my story!" I remember reading about the "Good Fight of Faith" in 1 Timothy 6:12, "Fight the good fight of the faith, lay hold on eternal life, to which you were called and have confessed the good confession in the presence of many witnesses (NKJV)." When your life hangs in the balance of life and death, there is a true spiritual battle going on.

During that time in my life, I trusted my Lord, Jehovah Rapha, to be Who He says He is, and I trusted Him for Healing!

Well, at each visit to the doctor, the tumor grew, and the cancer was very aggressive. When I looked at my situation, I remembered when David stepped on the field to face Goliath...he came in faith and trusted in the Lord. He declared that the battle belongs to the Lord! I read and recounted 1 Samuel 17; how young David did not have any fear facing the giant. Why? Because greater was the passion in him to stand against the giant who defied the Lord and the army of Israel. His perception was very different than his brothers. You see, David had been out in the field with the sheep when his father asked him to take food and nourishment to his brothers who were on the battlefield. When David saw that his brothers, along with all the army, were paralyzed in fear over the words spoken by this giant, they cowered and could not move.

Sometimes the enemy will taunt us too with words, to keep us paralyzed from moving in faith to trust and believe the Word of the Lord. David's heart trusted the Lord to be with him and face this giant! David knew *Who* he served, and he spoke and declared to the enemy he was facing that the battle belongs to the Lord!

I can remember sitting at the desk when the doctor had given me the report that I had a malignant tumor. It was a death sentence that my heart and spirit could not accept. I knew that the Lord was speaking to my heart, and when He speaks, His Word brings LIFE! I determined right then to trust God, no matter what!

When King Saul wanted to help David, he gave him his armor, but David could not fight this battle in someone else's armor. Be careful if you are fighting a battle and you want to see the mighty hand of God bring victory. You must be dressed in the armor of God that He has given you. Read Ephesians 6:10-18, for the Lord has equipped you with His armor to confront any battle that you may face. Let me ask you a question, when you get up in the morning, do you ever go out for the day without getting dressed?? NO! We would never do that…then why would we go each day without dressing ourselves in the armor of God? The armor of God will cause you to stand in your battle, steadfast; unmovable, knowing that the battle belongs to the Lord! He will not leave you; not now, not ever! His Word says in Hebrews 13:5, "…I will never leave you, nor forsake you (NKJV)." That is a promise!

I know that it was only God who could deliver me in this battle, so my hope and trust was completely in Him. I was so thankful for so many prayer warriors; especially my family, who joined me in believing God for my miracle, but it was God alone that I needed to move on my behalf. So, after months and months had gone by; the tumor growing in size and now evident on the back of my neck; my doctor called me into his office once again. I now sat in the same place where he had given me his initial bad report; he now declared there was nothing else that he could do for me. He said, "You need to go home and prepare for this cancer to take its course." He was truly giving me a death sentence! My husband had asked how long I had to live, and the doctor responded that it would be about SIX MONTHS, BUT NO MORE.

Again, I did not receive what he was telling me. At that moment, I felt an overwhelming PEACE come over me. I told the doctor, "Now I am in the Lord's hands and no one else's. He is the only One now that can help me." I must admit that right at that moment, my whole prayer life changed. Funny, isn't it? When you are desperate for God to do something, that you pray much differently than when everything is going well? I was at home for about one month, and during that time I sought Him like never before. I found that "Secret Place" and intimacy with my Father. He met me there and His Peace reassured me that He was in total control. I trusted His Word that I was in a "WIN – WIN" situation!! If the Lord decided to heal me, then He would show me victory over this cancer, but if it was His will to take me home, then I would see Him face to face!! <u>Either way, I WIN</u>! From that time on, I was filled with such love and passion for the Lord. It continually grows stronger, even today.

There was one Sunday, during that period of time, that I asked to go to church. I just felt that I needed to be there and hear the word. When my husband carried me into church, I sat on the back row all the way in the corner. Oh, and the Word spoken that day, I felt was just for me. The pastor spoke, "How desperate are you for God to move in your life today?" WOW, I thanked God for allowing me to be there. Yes, I was extremely weak; weighing about 96 pounds; no hair, but if *anyone* in that church was desperate for God to move that day, it was *me*. When the altar call came, so many people made their way to the altar for prayer. I thought I would be up there as well, but I was too weak and could not lift myself up. Well, until I heard the pastor say next, "For those of you still in your seats, if you can BELIEVE IN FAITH and pray with someone at this altar, please come and pray with them." Well, I got up like a rocket was stuck to my back, and I went straight to the altar to pray with a dear friend who was going through a devastating situation. I wanted to pray for her and her family. Pastor was going back and forth praying for everyone at the altar. He passed by many times and then when he prayed for everyone in the front, he went to the side of the altar by the window. Then the Lord spoke to him and said, "Go back, there's one more." When he started back across the front of the altar area, he stopped in front of me and raised his hand to pray – but he never touched me because I was further back and there were too many people in front of me.

I fell to the floor, overwhelmed with the Hand of the Lord touching me! I felt what seemed to be like warm oil covering my entire body. I thought that I was there for about one to two minutes. However, many eyewitnesses who stood there praying over me said I was there for over an hour! Wow, touched by the Hand of God! My husband took me back home and laid me in the bed. I fell into a sound sleep and when I awoke about 2 a.m., I first realized that I did not have a headache. This was significant because during this entire illness, I had constant headaches with no relief. There was so much pressure on my brain, but now, no pain!! When I put my hands on my head to feel the back of my neck where the tumor had been sticking out, I started thanking God because right then I realized that Jesus had done what He said He would do! THERE WAS NO TUMOR - INSTANTLY GONE! I praised God and thanked Him for this miraculous healing!

I had to wait until the next morning to call my doctor and let him know that Jesus had healed me, and that there was no more tumor. He asked me to come into the hospital so he could see me. I went, and he saw that there was no tumor there. He wanted to run a series of tests to make sure. Well, after all the tests were done, I went back to his office and the doctor now declared, "I DON'T KNOW WHAT HAPPENED, BUT THERE IS NO TUMOR AND NO CANCER!" I praised God and shared how the Lord had spoken the Word to my heart and did what only Jesus can do... "…with men this is impossible, but with God all things are possible." Matthew 19:26 (NKJV).

I realized that now I had a great work to go and do for the Lord. I sat up in my bed that night when I realized the tumor was gone, and I promised the Lord that for the rest of my life, I would go and do whatever He called me to do. I am so thankful that He continues to write my story even twenty-four years later. I find that it is even more exciting serving Him now than ever before. I am so passionately in love with Him and all that He has called me to do. I always want to make sure that He receives all the glory and all the honor in my life. All Glory to the miracle-working God who is willing and ready to heal you too today. DARE TO BELIEVE HIM!

Questions for Reflection

1. What is it that you are facing that you need the Lord to touch and heal today?

2. Do you need a miracle? Are you facing an impossible situation?

3. Do you know how to surrender completely to the Lord and His will?

4. How is your prayer life? Have you found the "secret place of the Most High"?

5. Do you desire a more intimate prayer time with the Lord?

6. Do you believe in the power of Almighty God and that He could turn your situation around for His glory?

Let us Pray

Abba Father, we bow in Your presence today. We come to give You praise, honor, and glory. We thank you for Your love, grace, and mercy. They are beyond measure for us. Lord, we look to You and ask that You would speak to our hearts right now, for You alone know exactly what each one is facing. We pray that as we surrender our will, may we cry out that Your Will be done in our hearts and in our lives. May we know Your voice so that when You speak, we will know that You are leading and guiding us according to Your perfect plan. Help us, dear Lord, when we are weak; to surrender and trust You. Fill us to overflowing with Your precious Holy Spirit and with blessings so that You may use us to be a blessing to all those we encounter. We speak healing right now to everyone who is sick in mind, body and spirit. We ask for a miracle today. We thank You, Lord, and give You all the honor and glory, in Jesus' Name. Amen.

Affirmations

- I believe in miracles

- I am healed

- I am optimistic

- I have hope

- Life in Christ is a WIN/WIN situation

- I believe in Jehovah Rapha – the God that heals

- All things are possible to those who believe – I Believe!

- I DARE TO BELIEVE!

Helpful Scriptures

- Matthew 19:26
- Psalm 103:2-3
- Isaiah 53:5
- 1 Peter 2:24
- Matthew 8:2-3
- Luke 4:40
- Luke 8:48
- Luke 5:15
- Mark 9:23

My Faith Steps

_____

_____

_____

_____

_____

_____

_____

_____

_____

_____

_____

CHAPTER 10

DECISION

TO

BELIEVE

Decision to Believe

Author Rhonda P. Fraser

Friends, this could be the most important chapter of your life! It could propel you to write your next chapter which could be a life-changing one.

In the introduction section of this book, I indicated that our lives are influenced by the choices we make. I also mentioned that just as we expect the maker of products and provider of services to deliver on their promises, we could rely on the promise of our Maker, Provider and Savior to get us to our destination. This chapter will demonstrate the application of those statements.

All the stories in this book have a common thread: we were all saved from a situation that was meant to destroy some aspect of our lives. There was an attack on our peace; health; relationships – purpose - mind, body, or soul. That is all the work of the enemy; the thief of our faith and soul. John 10:10 explains the enemy's work as one of destruction, but Jesus gives us abundant life.

The secret to facing the challenges of life is in a key decision that was made by every author of this book - the DECISION TO BELIEVE in GOD and yield to His sovereignty.

Our victories hinged upon our relationship with our all-powerful Lord, Jesus – the God of our salvation; not in our own strength. That is our most important foundational belief that has helped us to navigate the storms of life. He is the miracle-working God who is always ready to show His might and power to those who partner with Him. That means believing the message of salvation found in John 3:16, "For God so loved the world that He gave His Only Son, that whoever BELIEVES IN HIM should not perish but have everlasting life (NKJV)." It takes faith to believe the message of salvation.

Friends, everyone who gave their lives to the Lord, every Christian – follower of Christ - dared to believe that scripture! That is the dare that transforms and helps us to boldly walk through any journey assigned to our purpose. That is the resilient faith that makes everything possible and gives us peace in difficult times.

The exciting news is that there is room in the Kingdom of God for whoever needs it. It just requires that decision to believe and that step of faith to courageously walk towards it. If you are already a believer, I dare you to stand firm in your faith and believe God for even greater. If you have strayed from the faith, it is not too late to come back. His arms are opened wide. Make that decision today before time runs out. If you have never given your heart to the Lord, you too could respond to His urgent call and DARE TO BELIEVE in Him today. If you are not certain if any of this pertains to you, the following questions may help to guide your decision.

Questions for Reflection

1. Do you know that life continues after death, and that leg of the journey is the longer period - forever?

2. If you died today, do you know where you would spend eternity?

3. Do you know that everyone carries the breath of God, the same breath that He blew into the first man, Adam, which made him a living soul?

4. Do you know that everyone was born with a capacity within - our spirit, that connects back to that God who gave us that breath?

5. Do you understand that when we worship and praise God, our spirit is connecting back with Him? Do you know that is the only thing that He could use from us for Himself?

6. Do you know that if you are not worshipping God, you are **<u>definitely</u>** worshipping some other god attached to the enemy of your soul? That void is always filled with something. Even if you consider yourself an atheist, who does not believe in any god, you are still worshipping something – some "god". If you think you are a "Christian", whatever comes between you and God, is an idol that has

Resilient Faith: Dare to Believe

taken God's position in your life. It does not have to be a carving. It could even be a good thing that has become a god in your life. For example, it could be your relationships, possessions, job, hobby, money, intelligence, beauty, influence, "ministry" – accolades. It is anything that you value over God - anything that is occupying that sacred space within you that was designed for God. A good indication of what that god could be is to pay attention to how you spend your time and what constantly draws you – your adoration. That could be a good lead to your idol.

7. Do you feel empty on the inside, as if something is missing, even after you have fulfilled your natural desires?

8. Do you know that there is an enemy, the devil, that is vying for your soul to be with him in a lost eternity – in hell, that is the reason why you face those temptations - darkness? There is no neutral position. We are either serving God or serving the devil.

9. Do you know the John 3:16 story of salvation, where Jesus Christ died on a cross to redeem us back to God to spend all eternity with Him in Heaven when we leave this earth? He is our Lord and Savior. We hear it often at Easter time.

10. Do you want to know more about this story?

11. Are you willing to give Jesus a try - to fill that sacred place in your life that has been wrongfully occupied by the enemy with fleshly desires and darkness?

12. Do you know that it does not matter how many wrongs you have done, after you have given your life to Christ, He forgives you and gives you a brand you start? You become, what we call, a born-again believer. He continually forgives whenever we sincerely ask for forgiveness.

13. Would you like to make Him your Lord and Savior?

    If yes, sincerely say following prayer.

Let us Pray:

Prayer for Salvation

Heavenly Father, I come before you today in faith. I believe Your Son, Jesus Christ died on the cross to redeem my soul from the kingdom of darkness and destruction. I realize that I have sinned and I repent of every wrong that I have done and ask for your forgiveness. I now accept by faith, Jesus as my Lord and Savior. I renounce every tie with the devil and turn away from that old life. From this moment, I receive the gift of the Holy Spirit to help me serve and follow You to eternity. I declare it done, in the Name of Jesus. Amen!

Affirmations:

I AM FREE! I AM FORGIVEN! I AM SAVED! I AM NEW!

I DARE TO BELIEVE!

****

The Lord's Prayer

Our Father in heaven, hallowed be Your name. Your kingdom come. Your will be done on earth as it is in heaven. Give us this day our daily bread, and forgive us our debts, as we forgive our debtors, and do not lead us into temptation, but deliver us from the evil one. For Yours is the kingdom and the power and the glory forever. Amen!

Matthew 6:9-13 (NKJV)

If you sincerely said and believed that prayer of salvation, just like that you are now a born-again believer, a child of the Almighty God, and will spend eternity with Him, as long as you continue your faith walk with Him.

For everyone who is serious about the decision to believe; There is now obedience; turning away from the ways of the enemy and follow the Lord. It requires walking away from some situations that once held you captive. James 2:26 tells us "Faith without works is dead (NKJV)" which means intentional action is needed on our end. There is also now access to the Holy Spirit, our helper.

Jesus' death on the cross brought us salvation and many other benefits, including healing, deliverance, provision, and every good gift. Let us all believe and embrace everything that is available for us. We see this exemplified in the model prayer that Jesus gave us called the Lord's Prayer on the previous page. You could use that as a template for prayer for the various aspects of your life. The key components include: acknowledgment of God's sovereignty; requests for provision; forgiveness as we forgive others; protection against evil; glory, worship and praises to God. A good exercise is to write your own prayer from this model.

God expects us to live in a community. No one has life all figured out or could do it alone. We all need someone to help us through this journey. So, the next step is to develop your faith walk, not only through personal devotions, but with other believers, called the Body of Christ, the called-out ones, the church. That is the group of people that the Lord is returning for one day. That is the next big event to come that we cannot afford to miss!

It is time to tell others the "Good News" – the news of salvation. How sad to experience a beautiful eternity with Jesus while others have to go to a lost eternity. So many are caught up with just materialism but lack that inner peace that Jesus gives. Romans 8:36-37 presents a very troubling question: "what will it profit a man if he gains the _whole world_, and loses his soul? …what will a man give in exchange for his soul (NKJV)?"

I implore you that nothing in the world is more precious than giving your soul to the Lord. Everything outside of Him is an empty shell with no peace, no true substance or value. Yes, there is no guarantee that everyone we encounter will believe or make it to Heaven, and that is the most heartbreaking statement. However, we cannot save anyone or make that decision for them. Everyone has to make that decision on their own. That is why we should be happy to share our faith with others and pray for them. That is the reason we wrote this book; to give you an opportunity to believe and to offer you a tool to give to someone who seems to have lost their way – lost their faith. This could probably be one of the best gifts you could ever give to someone – a message of Faith, Hope, and Love in Jesus! (1 Corinthians 13:13).

Friends, at back of this book, you will see blank pages. These are good reminders that every time we sincerely repent, God gives us a new page – a clean, fresh start. Regardless of how many wrong turns you have made in life, today is always the opportunity to write a new chapter. You get to decide how you will start the new chapter of your life. Take that step of faith and start writing your new story today. God is right there waiting to help you on this new exciting journey! Make it a good one! Love You!

Helpful Scriptures

- Hebrews 7:25

- 2 Corinthians 5:17

- Ephesians 2:8

- Galatians 2:16

- John 5:24

- Acts 4:12

- 1 John 4:9

- Romans 3:23

- Romans 6:23

- John 6:35

- 2 Peter 3:9

My Prayer

_____

_____

_____

_____

_____

_____

_____

_____

_____

_____

My Faith Steps

_____

_____

_____

_____

_____

_____

_____

_____

_____

_____

_____

My Affirmations

_____

_____

_____

_____

_____

_____

_____

_____

_____

Affirmations

I AM CHOSEN

I AM WHOLE

I AM FREE

I AM HOPEFUL

I AM SPECIAL

I AM WORTHY

I AM BLESSED

I AM FAVORED

I AM HEALED

I AM DELIVERED

I AM FORGIVEN

I AM LOVED

I AM SAVED

ABOUT THE AUTHORS

Rhonda P. Fraser, MBA
Min./Empowerment Speaker

Rhonda considers Her Christian Faith the most important aspect of her life. She was baptized at age thirteen in Guyana, South America, where she was born and has been fulfilling the leadership calling of God on her life, primarily is New York, since the nineties.

She resides in Long Island, New York with her family. She has been married to her husband, Rev. Reginald Fraser since 1988. They have three beautiful children, Raphael, Reginald Jr., Rebecca (R. Frasers). Spending time with them brings her much joy. They have made valuable investments in sharing their talent in music, worship, leadership, and overall empowerment to churches, organizations, and individuals, primarily in New York for decades. She is an anointed worship leader.

Rhonda is a personal development and leadership coach. She also functions in various leadership roles, including, CEO of R. Fraser Consulting Services and CEO of R. Frasers Connection, LLC. She is an influential women's leader who has been the Women's Ministry Rep.; Worship/Youth Leader; Advisor and Social Needs Connection for over 30 organizations, including churches, in New York. She is an empowerment specialist and has been the speaker at dynamic women empowerment conferences for a number of years.

Writing is her passion. She is a bestselling author for the following inspirational books which she co-authored:

1. Women of War: Peace in the Midst of Storm (Compiler Dr. D. Musielak)

2. This Is How I Fight My Battles (Compiler K. Etwaru)

Rhonda is also the lead author and compiler of the following 2021 book releases:

1. Resilient Faith: Dare to Believe

2. Empowered to Overcome Tough Season of Life

She also a contributing author for two books "*The Professional Woman*" for Professional Women Network (PWN) to be released in 2021. Her P.U.S.H Guidebook which she uses for her women's conferences is also scheduled to be released in 2021. She also wrote several empowerment pieces for conferences, ministry women magazines *(The Encourager)*, and other online motivational pieces.

Rhonda is a Corporate Finance, Marketing and Strategy Expert, with a Master's Degree (MBA), specialization in Strategic Management, Finance, and Marketing from Villanova University.

She is gifted with connecting people from all backgrounds and integrates her strategy expertise with her ministry. Her overall goal is to be a servant-leader, to live a balanced life – spiritually, physically, mentally, and emotionally and empower others (especially women) to do the same.

Contact Information:

Websites:

rfraserconsulting.com

rfrasersconnection.com

rhondafraser.com

rfrasersempowermentnetwork.com

Online Store: payhip.com/RFraser

Facebook: Rhondapfraser

RFrasers Empowerment Network

Instagram: @rhondapfraser

Twitter: @Rhondapfraser

Carol L. Brown
Chaplain/Pastor

Carol L. Brown was born and raised in Brooklyn, NY and has known the Lord Jesus as her personal savior for 39 years.

She studied at Baruch College in New York City where she earned a Bachelor's Degree in Sociology/Social Work, and was elected president of her Intervarsity Christian Fellowship chapter on campus.

The Lord placed a burden in Carol's heart at a young age for foreign missions and she answered the call by taking short term missionary trips to Belgium in Europe, Ghana in West Africa, Kenya in East Africa and Jamaica West Indies, spreading His gospel.

Carol attended New York Christian Counseling Center, New York City, where she earned a Pastoral Care Certificate–Completion of course of study of Temperament Therapy. Carol recently earned a certificate in Biblical Counseling.

Carol presently serves as an assistant pastor at Huntington Assembly of God as well as a Chaplain under NYS Chaplaincy Task Force.

Carol headed up Youth ministry for many years, served in various roles in Women's Ministry including president, and various roles of church administration.

Professionally she works for Developmental Disabilities Institute, serving adults in this population.

Carol has been married to her loving husband Robert for 29 years. He is an ordained Assemblies of God pastor and together they share a deep passion to serve the Lord. They have three daughters Rochelle, Jewel and Ashley and reside in West Babylon, NY.

Contact Information:

www.Carollbrown.com

JoAnne Eronini, MS
Min./First Lady

JoAnne M. Eronini was born in Richmond, Virginia and now resides in Staten Island, New York with her family. JoAnne is a mother and the wife of Rev. Ed Chi-Eronini, pastor of new church plant, Vertical Christian Center (www.vccsiny.com). As part of their mission to reach the world, they provide missionary support to an orphanage in Nigeria.

She is a Proverbs 31 woman who manages her Christian life and professional life guided by her strong passionate belief and love for God. She has functioned in various leadership and ministry roles, and is a woman of many talents:

She is a retired military personnel of 23 years and a former school teacher with special education population for eight years. She now works in the mental health field.

JoAnne received her undergraduate degree from Norfolk State University and her Master's Degree in Counseling from New York University.

She is also a licensed cosmetologist in New York. Her passion is to use this talent to show God's love to the elderly population.

Her passion is seeing lives transformed and realizing God is the answer!

Contact Information:

Website: Joanneeronini.com

Online Store: payhip.com/JChiMart

JoAnne can also be reached at Vertical Christian Center on fb and website.

Crystal Lodico
Missionary

Raised to follow life guidelines, go to college, get a job, and make money. I moved out to New York City, completed a BA in Communications only to find myself unfulfilled. Hungry for a purpose, I waved Bon Voyage to everything I thought would make me happy; recommitted my life to following Jesus. It was not easy, but since then, I have answered YES to the call for missions and the Lord has been taking me across borders to help bridge the gap between media and missions.

In El Salvador, I will be serving with Kings Castle Ministries. My role will include leading teams in evangelistic ministry, working with children, and joining their media team to help share the testimonies of lives transformed by the gospel.

Contact Information:

Crystallodico@gmail.com

Instagram: @cryslodico

Facebook: Crys Lodico

Website: Livinginpeaces.com

Evelyn P. Andrews
Elder

Eight-four-year-old Evelyn P. Andrews is the mother of three beautiful daughters, six grandchildren and one great grandson.

She was born in Guyana and followed Jesus from her young adult years. She further strengthened her faith walk in the eighties after she was baptized by Bishop John Cummings at Newtown AOG church. She continues to serve God passionately.

Evelyn is a typical behind the scenes stalwart of the faith – "war room" elder! Called to the ministry of intercession, especially for leaders, she commits a lot of her time to prayer and encouraging others in the faith. She is a key prayer support to her daughter Rhonda, especially for her women empowerment ministry.

She resides in Long Island, New York and spends some of her time in the United Kingdom.

Her talents include cosmetology, fashion designing/ seamstress, craft-making, gardening and exceptional culinary skills.

Spending time with her grandchildren is the highlight of her days. They keep her young and energized. She enjoys reading.

Her passion is seeing souls saved, which has given her the drive to share her faith stories with others. In addition to this book, some of these stories are found in the following books:

1. *Empowered to Overcome Tough Seasons of Life. (Compiled by Rhonda P. Fraser)* Evelyn is a co-author of this book.

2. *Women of War: Peace in the Midst of the Storm (Compiled by Dr. Delene Musielak)* Her story is shared by Author Rhonda P. Fraser

Contact Information:
Website: Evelynpandrews.com

Online Store: Payhip.com/EPAndrews

Heather Barfield

Pastor

Pastor Heather Barfield is a retired school teacher and mother of two adult sons.

She has been ministering the Word of God for over twenty-five years. She has taught God's Word to all ages and has seen lives transformed through the reading and study of the Word of God.

Pastor Barfield speaks, ministers, preaches, and teaches at various events including women's conferences, prayer retreats, church functions, and women's meetings. She hosts annual women conferences through her ministry, Daughters of Destiny, in which she enables, equips, and encourages women to enter into their divinely appointed destinies.

She operates in a strong prophetic anointing, and God uses her to speak life into the lives of woman who have been battered or abused physically, mentally, emotionally, and spiritually.

Pastor Barfield is also the author of two books: *Meeting God Daily*, a 52-week devotional designed to bring the reader into a closer walk with God and her second book *The Well Woman* [Revised Edition] which takes the reader on a life-changing journey of healing and restoration.

Both books are available on Amazon or they may be ordered at her website.

Contact Information:

Website: <u>heatherbarfieldministries.com</u>.

Marsha Winters
Missionary

Marsha has been married for over twenty years to Samuel Winters with four beautiful children. Samuel has been the Associate Pastor for their church for over fourteen years, and now Marsha and Samuel are local missionaries for the AG.

Marsha and her husband have ministered full-time to thousands of youths, women, men, couples and children's ministry through preaching, teachings and workshops.

In their time serving others, they realized that there were many who struggled as Marsha did, so in 2015 they wrote a book based around her testimony of surviving severe physical and sexual abuse called, *The Threshing: A Weapon Forged by Fire*, and their second book, *The Threshing: The Makings of a Soldier*. After writing those books, Samuel and Marsha were led to start a non-for-profit organization called Through the Winters Ministry. They help those that have gone through trauma, loss, abuse or grief, to find purpose in their pain.

Her deepest desire to share the love of God in any way possible; showing God's faithfulness even through the hardest seasons of life.

Contact Information:

Website: throughthewinters.com

Heather Meyerend
Elder

Heather Meyerend is convinced that the seasons of our life are opportunities that God uses to manifest His glory and bring us to a deeper understanding of divine everyday purpose

Heather is a recently retired Hospice nurse who now embraces a new season of creativity and spending leisurely time with God.

Heather is an Elder and member of Christian Heritage Church in Brooklyn, NY where she serves as a teacher and in a new role as Mission Director under Bishop Albert C. Delmadge and his wife Pastor Merna Delmadge.

She has always loved the outdoors and enjoys gardening, hiking and summer adventures with her husband, Paul. She is the mother of two amazing young adults, David and Danny, who are on their way to accomplishing great things for the Kingdom of God.

Contact Information:

Website: Heathermeyerend.com

Eileen Howarth
Reverend/Pastor

Rev. Eileen M. Howarth was born and raised in Brooklyn, New York. She is married to husband, James. They are blessed with a son, David; daughter, Milena; their wonderful spouses and four beautiful granddaughters.

Eileen was saved in June, 1985 at Calvary Assembly of God in Staten Island, NY. She currently serves as Associate Pastor there.

She has an amazing testimony of how God performed a miracle in healing her from brain cancer after the doctors gave her six months to live 1996.

The Lord has opened doors, all over the world, for her to testify of God's healing touch and to bring His Word of encouragement and faith to all those who would believe God for the impossible in their lives.

She is a Licensed Minister with the Assemblies of God and has ministered in Israel; London; Spain; Italy; Ireland and all over the United States and Latin America. She has served over 13 years in the mission field helping to build churches in Haiti; Dominican Republic; Chile; Ghana Africa, Montreal and Puerto Rico. She has taught and lead teams to minister in each of these countries.

Discipling and training those that are passionate about serving our Lord and Savior. She leads a thriving ministry of women who love to serve the Lord!

Her desire is to be surrendered to the Lord's calling and He alone be glorified!

Contact Information:

Website: Eileenhowarth.com

Notes

_____

_____

_____

_____

_____

_____

_____

_____

_____

_____

Notes

_____

_____

_____

_____

_____

_____

_____

_____

_____

_____

Notes

_____

_____

_____

_____

_____

_____

_____

_____

_____

_____

Notes

_____

_____

_____

_____

_____

_____

_____

_____

_____

_____

Notes

_____

_____

_____

_____

_____

_____

_____

_____

_____

_____

Made in the USA
Middletown, DE
28 November 2021